Game Winning Goals
Hockey's Best Kept Secrets
For Parents, Players & Coaches

Daryl Jenner

Published by: Profits Publishing
http://profitspublishing.com/

US Address

1300 Boblett Street,
Blaine WA, 98230

Phone: 866-492-6623
Fax: 250-493-6603

Canadian Address

1265 Charter Hill Drive
Coquitlam, BC, V3E1P1

Phone: 604-941-3041
Fax: 604-944-7993

Game Winning Goals
Hockey's Best Kept Secrets
For Parents, Players & Coaches

Copyright 2009 By Daryl Jenner

All Rights Reserved

First Printing: September 2009

ISBN: 978-1-933817-46-0

I would like to personally thank and recognize the efforts of several people that have made this book possible.

James Dewer, Game Action Photo. Responsible for the book's cover and several of the photos throughout the book, plus all my website design, www.yougottalovethisgame.com

Jeff McCallum, Bob Burnham at **Expert Author Publishing.com** , for all their consulting and support, helping this book become a reality, if you are thinking of writing a book, these are the guys to speak to.

Kirk Lamb athletic advisor for the AJHL, his information on Scholarships is invaluable, every year the requirements change so use this information as a guide only. Talk to your guidance counselor or contact Kirk Lamb at advisor@ajhl.ca

All photos were taken by Game action photo except where noted. Every reasonable attempt was made to give proper credit. If there are any errors, please notify the publisher and corrections will be made in subsequent additions.

I would also like to acknowledge the many people from who have helped me develop into the person I am today.
Tim Coghlin, Head Coach St Norbert College NCAA, Saul Miller, professional motivational speaker, Alan Kerr VP Okanagan Hockey School, Richard Kromm Head Coach Muskegan Lumberjacks IHL, Larry Lund Founder Okanagan Hockey School, Blake Wesley Okanagan Hockey Academy Junior Coach, Richard Anderson BC Best Ever District Evaluator, Geoff Goodman Junior Flames Lacrosse Coach, John Lee Kootnekoff professional motivational speaker, Dixon Ward Director of hockey operations Okanagan Hockey School, Jeff Thorburn Kelowna Rockets Head Trainer,

HOCKEY DEVELOPMENT CAMPS

Gerry Marsh Goaltending Consultant, Jamie Watts, Former Head Instructor Okanagan Hockey Schools, Barry Smith, Kamloops Blazers Head Coach, Heather Chartres former Penticton Panthers Trainer, Don McCall OHS Instructor, Darren Wilms Professional Yoga Instructor, Fred Dobransky, OHS Scout, Justin Keller Norfolk Admirals AHL, Darren Jensen Former Philadelphia Flyers Goalie, Steve O'Rourke Assistant Coach Abbotsford Heat AHL, Bryant Perrior Albernie Valley Bulldogs Head Coach, Alan Hicks Reddeer Coach, Kolin Kennedy Hockey Goalie Coach, Bryan Kitchen GM Summerland Warriors, Nila Reinboldt IDT Rep, Mike Kelly President Texas Minor Hockey, Tom Bohmer Quesnel Millionaire Head Coach, Aaron Nell England Professional League, Steve Nell GM England Professional league, Roland Habisroutinger Professional Agent and Scout, Randy Kaylnuk Manitoba Coach, Dan Noble WHL Scout, Ernie Bone BC Best Ever Coach, Bernie Pimm BC Best Ever Coach, Dave Zarn Trainer Victoria Salmon Kings ECHL,

www.yougottalovethisgame.com

www.designerhockeydrills.com

Testimonials

I met Daryl in 2000 at a hockey school in British Columbia, Canada. Daryl was assigned to coach the team we brought from Dallas, Texas. We competed for two weeks in an International Hockey Tournament that also included two weeks of hockey instruction. I learned more about coaching during the two weeks I observed Daryl coach the team during the tournament games and the lessons he taught the team during the camp sessions than all the previous years I had coached. He is an excellent teacher and communicator. Daryl is a coach and an individual that can relate not only to the kids on the team but more importantly to the coaches also. Daryl is an individual of the highest integrity and character. I continue to seek his advice whenever the situation dictates.
Michael Kelly, Dallas Texas
President, Dallas Metro Hockey Association
Southlake, Texas

Knowing Daryl Jenner has certainly been an experience and indeed a pleasure. In the midst of the highly competitive world of hockey, Daryl has worn many hats, and he has done it successfully. Throughout the 10 years our son has played hockey, Daryl has been the coach who has had the most positive influence in his life on and off the ice. Daryl's knowledge of the game and more important his ability to coach and relate to the kids makes him a huge success, not only with the kids, but the parents as well. We have watched Daryl coach Atoms to Jr's, and at each level he has demonstrated to us that he has what it takes to develop the whole player.
Julie Roskosh
Albuquerque
New Mexico

I have known Darryl Jenner for a number of years. Daryl and I worked for several years in the hockey world and I have watched the man coach, motivate and promote players to the next level, he organize tournaments, and control all aspects of a major hockey organization. Daryl Jenner is a dependable, reliable, hard working, and conscientious person. It was an honor for myself to be involved with Daryl and we have become good friends over the past years. I wish Daryl the best of health and happiness.
Fred Dobransky
Penticton B.C.

Daryl has been extremely helpful with his advice and insight as my son progressed from the Bantam level to Junior Hockey.
John Dowling
Calgary Alberta

I had the opportunity to work with Daryl for many years at the Okanagan Hockey School. Daryl is an outstanding student of the game of Hockey. His attitude Instruction and coaching skills are among the best in the game. This is proven as he was a head instructor and ran the highly successful International Development Tournament at the Okanagan Hockey School for many years, and did a first class job of it. He was also a coach/Instructor for the Okanagan Hockey Academy several years where he was well liked and respected by his players, parents and staff. It was a real pleasure to work alongside such a quality individual.

Don McCall
Retired OHA, OHS Instructor from 1970-2007

I have had the pleasure of knowing Daryl for the past 5 years and coaching with him for 2 of those 5 years. As a coach, Daryl creates highly effective practice plans for all phases of the game teaching offensive, defensive and special team concepts in a logical progression. Daryl has the uncanny ability of making all players, regardless of their abilities, an integral part of the team. TEAM is the main concept he teaches, making it fun for all. As a student of the game Daryl works tirelessly and selflessly to help his players enhance their skills as hockey players but more importantly as people. As a fellow coach I have learned a lot from working with Daryl and have been able to transfer his knowledge to the sport of lacrosse.

Geoff Goodman
Head Coach, South Okanagan Flames Jr. Lacrosse Club

Daryl has been a lifelong friend and I value his insight and opinion. As a hockey player, coach and now father of a young player he has a great perspective on the game. Daryl works as a regional scout for St Norbert and is a tremendous evaluator of talent and character.

Tim Coghlin
Head Coach St Norbert College
NCAA Champions 2008

I had the pleasure of meeting Daryl Jenner at the Okanagan Hockey school in the summer of 2004. I have been putting teams together for hockey tournaments for about 8 years now and I was very impressed with Daryl's character, knowledge, and dedication to the game! He invited Kenny to participate in the IDT which was a great experience. Daryl coached Kenny for some of his first year at OHA. He definitely has a lot of knowledge and is a very good motivator. He really cares about the kid's development and encourages them to be of good character on the ice as well as off the ice. He is a great guy who really cares about all of the kids he has ever coached!

Michael Whitford
Fort McMurry AB

It has been more than a pleasure to have crossed paths with Daryl Jenner he has been the inspiration with a solid kick of reality for our son Ryan. It was Daryl's keen eye on base skills and acute sense of Ryan's grit and determination that propelled our son to the Junior A hockey ranks. A level of hockey that many, of the so called experienced coaches, said he would never reach. Daryl's ability to see and analyze a player's talent is remarkable, our son has had the opportunity to play all over North America, from Texas to Boston, from Denver to Las Vegas and there has only been one place that he has come away with more knowledge and confidence, that is when he skated with Daryl in Penticton, B.C.

Daryl has not only been a coach for Ryan but a visionary, he sees more in players than they see in themselves. More importantly he helps them build the confidence they need to believe in his vision. This is a talent that too many coaches today boast they have, but in reality they lack. I confidently believe that Daryl's mantra for success revolves around the concept that 'it is not how high you climb the ladder of success but how many you bring with you on the climb'. Daryl from our family and especially from our son Ryan we thank you for all you have done, from on the ice coaching to on the phone pep talks, Ryan is truly a better person and hockey player because of you.
Scott and Karla Townsend
Las Vegas Nevada

Daryl Jenner has been a big influence on my hockey career from the first time I stepped on the ice with him five years ago. Daryl's knowledge of the game is a big reason why he is able to be such an affective coach. The drills, plays, and hockey sense I have learned from Daryl have kept with me throughout my playing and coaching career. The one thing I have found that separates Daryl from other coach's is his approach to the game, while I worked hard and learned a lot every time I was on the ice with Daryl he always found a way to keep it fun.
Hans Roskosh
Albuquerque
New Mexico

As much as Daryl has a vast knowledge of the game; His best trait has been his approach to the game, he seems to be able to get the best out of his players while keeping the game fun. While being firm with all the players he has taught he still earns complete respect of his athletes. Daryl is definitely a player's coach.
Gerry Marsh
Summerland B.C

Because of Daryl's coaching and book, my son's skating ability has increased by 50% and has   gone from scoring a few goals to being one of the top point's leaders on his team. Thanks Daryl!
Jeff McCallum
Summerland B.C.

I have had the pleasure of knowing Daryl Jenner for the last ten years and the honor of coaching with him for five of those years.

Daryl's commitment and dedication as a hockey coach is second only to his love and passion for his family and children. While at the rink, Daryl shows tremendous work ethic and devotion to his players, he is truly a player's coach who commands the respect and gets the most of those who play for him. He creates a very positive learning environment, and he ensures that the most important aspect of the game is not forgotten, the players have fun.

During my time working with Daryl, I travelled extensively with him and was very impressed by his dedication as a father. His family and children were always a part of each day and to see them interact together was truly awe inspiring and humbling as a person. I believe that anyone can learn from the example that Daryl demonstrates showing an unmatched passion for both the game of hockey and his family.

Jamie Watts
Former Head Instructor
Okanagan Hockey School

The Author reminds us that the Wayne Gretzky's, Sidney Crosby's, Steven Nash's do not evolve out of fear, rejection and greed… they are empowered because of unconditional love by nurturing from creative parents, teachers, and coaches. Daryl's book is timely and meaningful!

John Lee Kootnekoff
Parent, professional coach, author
Inspirational and motivational speaker at the World Famous Okanagan Hockey School for 25 consecutive years

Daryl was a positive influence throughout my young minor hockey career, also helping me make the jump from Junior B to Junior A. Daryl is a knowledgeable hockey figure and makes the game fun to play.

Justin Keller
Norfolk Admirals
American Hockey League

I met Daryl 2 seasons before Midget at an IDT. He helped me get my level up and he coached me part of my first year of Midget! He helped me settle in to a higher level of hockey than I was used to. I learned allot about the mental part of the game from him. He is one of my most favorite coaches I have ever had. He is a great guy and coach!

Kenny Whitford
Fort McMurry Alberta

Our Drill Designer Program will give you all the drills and information that you will need to make up quality practice plans and be able to execute these plans to perfection, you can get more information on our drill site at www.designerhockeydrills.com

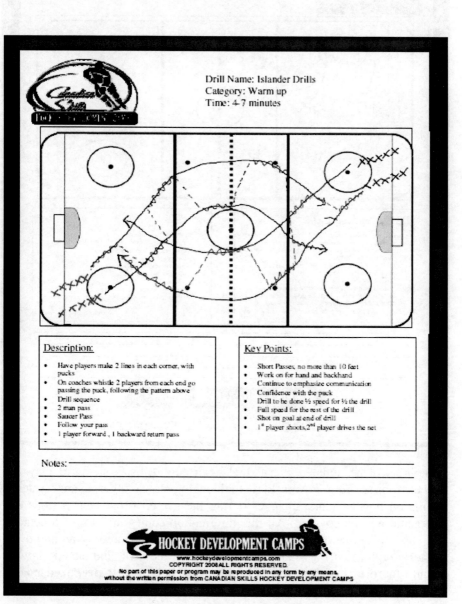

Drill Name: Islander Drills
Category: Warm up
Time: 4-7 minutes

Description:

- Have players make 2 lines in each corner, with pucks
- On coaches whistle 2 players from each end go passing the puck, following the pattern above
- Drill sequence
- 2 man pass
- Saucer Pass
- Follow your pass
- 1 player forward , 1 backward return pass

Key Points:

- Short Passes, no more than 10 feet
- Work on for hand and backhand
- Continue to emphasize communication
- Confidence with the puck
- Drill to be done ½ speed for ½ the drill
- Full speed for the rest of the drill
- Shot on goal at end of drill
- 1st player shoots, 2nd player drives the net

Notes:

HOCKEY DEVELOPMENT CAMPS

HOCKEY SKILLS
DESIGNER DRILLS

Drill Name: Penalty Kill FC
Category: Primary
Time:

Description: High T ,FC

- F1 steers player coming out from behind the net, his job is to make him deliver the out let pass to the wall, and once he passes the puck, F1 then back checks up the middle of the ice with speed.
- F2 Sets up high, about 10 feet inside the blue line, once he reads the direction of the for check. he 1st takes away the stretch pass up the middle of the ice, he then jumps to the puck where the pass is going. If the puck is turned over , he dumps the puck back deep and resets for check. D1 and D2 cover stretch pass, and always keep the puck in front of them.

Key Points:

- Team communication
- Quickness to the puck
- Hard work in all areas of the ice
- Simple plays
- Quick and intelligent changes
- Never check behind the net
- Active stick
- Must be committed to team play
- F1 must be quick back up ice, do not take yourself out of the play to make a hit.

Notes:

HOCKEY DEVELOPMENT CAMPS

This Site will be updated every week with new drills, systems of play and various topics, from Power Play to breaking down other teams systems. Details on how to make changes during the game, in between periods and post game will be covered. All this information comes in form of a detailed drill sheet as above, plus each drill or topic is accompanied by an audio file going through the drill, what to look for within the drill, and exactly how to execute the drill to perfection .**The best coach is a well prepared coach.** Visit us at **www.designerhockeydrills.com**

TABLE OF CONTENTS

INTRODUCTION

Hockey has always been a very big part of my life. Whether it was watching Hockey Night in Canada with my dad or playing street hockey with my friends, I always pictured myself scoring the Stanley Cup winning goal or making a big save to preserve the win! These kinds of dreams will always be the cornerstone of Canadian Hockey. Going to the rink at 6:00am without fail and trying to get on the ice as early as the rink attendant would let us. The game of hockey has always been about the KIDS. But to this point, I don't think people realize the importance of the parent's role in their child's hockey development in either a positive or negative way. That's right, I said it! Negative. I have spent over 20 years coaching players at various levels, and 20 years playing the game from minor hockey to junior. Over the years I have seen and heard a lot of shocking things at the rink.

With regards to my coaching experience, I was fortunate to work with several professionals that taught me that being a coach did not just mean teaching the game itself, but also to instill, Integrity, Honesty, and Character into each athlete. These are traits that will be utilized the rest of their lives, even if they don't play in the NHL. Through my career I found that easiest player's to work with had parents that were open-minded and supportive of the coach and the rest of the volunteers. Hockey is a diversified sport that is very emotional at all levels on and off the ice, but it wasn't until I followed my son's hockey as a parent that I realized parental emotions also run very deep. Things that were said in the stands made me want to be back behind the bench. We all love our kid's dearly and want the best for them, but are we really doing the right thing for our young athletes by being so involved? In this book I will shed some light on the Game and how you as parents, can have a positive influence on your son or daughter's hockey development.

CHAPTER 1
MAKING THE MOST OF YOUR CHILD'S FIRST YEAR IN HOCKEY

A s with all sports that we enter our children in, the main theme in hockey is to always have fun, do something to stay active, but not necessarily to make the NHL, or become an Olympian. But now that your child has chosen to play the game of hockey, what's next? Kids, when they decide to play hockey, see only one thing, the stick and the puck. No thought is ever put on the most important part of the game, skating. It is your job to incorporate the two. First and foremost, the key for all young hockey players is to learn how to skate. The main objective when teaching your child to skate is to make it FUN and be creative in your approach.

HOCKEY DEVELOPMENT CAMPS

There are probably several learn to skate programs in your local community but there is no substitute for dear old dad or mom taking their child to public skating, and helping him or her along with the basic skill of just staying up on their feet. An organized program that I found in Summerland, B.C. Canada, had the beginning players wear their hockey equipment to the practices. They would be on the ice twice a week, with the practices divided into two distinct halves.

The first half of each practice focused strictly on skating skills without the use of sticks. The second half of the practice would focus on basic skill development using their sticks. The idea to spend the first half of practice with no sticks is very important for the young player. The players are now forced to skate with no crutch, allowing them to focus on balance and stride. Parents know that skating is the cornerstone for any good hockey player, but keep it FUN and POSITIVE.

One recurring question that I have been asked while working with the Okanagan Hockey School is: How early in life should I have my son or daughter on the ice? The answer I always give: The earlier the better, BUT they must be physically and mentally ready for this very difficult challenge. My son Dawson went on the ice for the first time when he was 3 and we found out right away that was too early for him. Every player is different in confidence and ability. The main question is, will they enjoy their experience on the ice and will they want to do it again? If they want to play hockey, get them a net and a stick so they can play the game on the driveway at home. They will be in a comfortable environment and be able to have some success just playing with the puck or ball. Several years ago Wayne Gretzky said that one of the things missing in today's game is the time spent playing pickup hockey in a back yard rink. The last few years I have worked as an assistant coach with the Okanagan Hockey Academy in Penticton, British Columbia, and one of our main philosophies has been spending a lot of time working on the fundamentals of the game away from the rink. Shooting pucks, passing, and stick handling off the ice as part of our daily dry land. We also put a lot of emphasis on agility work with a stick and puck, skills also done away from the rink, with players as old as 17! This is an example of how valuable time off the ice can be time used in developing player's hockey skills.

HOCKEY DEVELOPMENT CAMPS

It is very important to introduce your son or daughter to the game at an early age, but they need to be confident and ready to take on the challenge of learning to skate. If it is at 3, 4, 5, or 6 years of age, don't worry, he or she will pick up the skill much easier if they are physically ready to learn it.

Before your son or daughter ever steps on the ice, another key concern must be the safety of your child. Injuries, particularly concussions, are the main cause of hockey players leaving the game before they want to. Concussions are a result of a blow to the head, either by a stick, puck, body check, or contact with the boards. Goalies are extremely susceptible to head injuries for obvious reasons. The black disc that we all love to chase can become a missile when shot by a good player or even the beginner player, who can get a hold of one once in a while.

So you parents, if your child wants to try the game or just wants to learn to skate, buy a new, quality approved concussion proof helmet. They can cost upwards of $200 dollars. I know what you are thinking. What if my child only plays for a year, or even worse, what if he or she decides they don't like the sport at all? Here is the truth of the matter, if you are willing to let your child partake in Canada's favorite pastime knowing full well that hockey is an expensive sport, do yourself favor. Be intelligent and start with the essentials. Helmet first, then Skates.

When purchasing skates, always buy new and make sure they are fitted properly by a local sports shop professional. If you really want to see your child have a great experience, do not be talked into buying an oversized skate that will last them for a couple of seasons. For starters, your child will end up with cold feet and be uncomfortable on the ice making their experience very unpleasant, and might discourage him or her from wanting to go out again. This can be prevented with a little knowledge and letting the sales person know exactly what you want. You are not suiting up your child to play hockey for the future, you are protecting them from harm by getting them proper fitting equipment that will help them have a great experience on the ice. When they grow out of their skates, buy them another proper fitting set. Several stores offer a trade in value to take away the sting of buying new skates year after year, a question that you will want to ask your sales rep before purchasing your first set of skates.

So, at this point you are thinking that I am a salesman for a local sports company! This is a conclusion that couldn't be further from the truth. After a good helmet and skates, the rest of the gear can be purchased used at a hockey swap or if you are fortunate enough to be able to afford the new gear, go nuts, just make sure you buy everything that fits them TODAY. Again, as stated above, don't buy oversized equipment.

Here is a guideline on shopping for your first set of equipment. Once you buy a new helmet and skates, talk to your local sports store expert, they

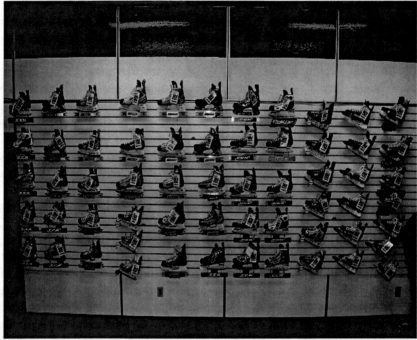

will be willing to spend some time with you as you have already made a couple of major purchases. Then you can discuss the rest of the gear with the salesman and try it on to find out exactly what size your child needs. Believe it or not the sports stores are there to help you, especially when you have already made a significant purchase. Trust me this works.

Once you are educated on the size of equipment your child needs. Then you can go to a hockey swap meet, or look in the local paper for the right size equipment with confidence. The general guideline for fitting your child is very simple. Following is a snapshot of what to look for in your child's first set of hockey gear. If you purchase used gear, make sure the equipment is clean, or have it cleaned and sterilized, this will take away any bad odor and help with the life of the equipment. This is a simple process, and again if you are trying to save money, smelly hockey gear, even if it is quality equipment, is going to be cheaper to purchase for obvious reasons, so don't be afraid to buy it, just have it cleaned.

SKATES

When buying <u>hockey skates</u>, you can basically throw your shoe size out the window. Each hockey skate is unique and <u>hockey skate manufacturers</u> seem to have their own method of sizing. Don't worry if you wear a size 10 shoe and a size 8 skate. That's pretty common as skate sizes are generally smaller. Just worry about wearing ones that fit. You need to make sure you have the right length and width boot to ensure the skates are comfortable.

HOW DO I KNOW IF MY SKATES ARE THE RIGHT SIZE?

You should make sure your toes do not touch the end of the skate. You should be able to comfortably wiggle them. Also make sure your heel does not slip up in the boot. Make sure the sides of your feet are comfortable and are not being pinched. If they are, ask your skate professional to size you in a skate that comes in a wider fit. There are many variables and sizes to skates.

IS IT OKAY TO BUY A PAIR OF SKATES THAT ARE A SIZE OR TWO BIGGER THAN THE ATHLETE'S FEET, ASSUMING THAT THEY WILL GROW INTO THEM?

You should never buy skates that are too big for any player, especially a beginner, as it will drastically hamper their skating ability and will lead to an unpleasant skating experience. Remember this is the first time your son or daughter hits the ice, there experience will leave a long lasting impression directly on how much he/she may actually like the sport. Spend the money in the right areas; your players will thank you for it. Get wood sticks, buy used equipment, save the money in these areas and then do the right thing, go buy proper fitting new skates and a quality new helmet. This skate sizing chart on the next page, is available at most of your local sporting good stores. Be aware that this chart is strictly a reference guide and will only get you close to the size that you may actually wear. Skates always should be purchased by feel and comfort, not brand name. What you see on television is just company's endorsing there brand. Professional hockey players don't all wear the same brand of skate. As a matter of fact, every major skate manufacturer has players in the NHL wearing their brand of skate. Be wise in your selection process, try on several pairs and get the skate's that feel the best on your feet, period.

Men's US Shoe Size	Bauer, CCM, Mission, Graf, Tour & Easton		Ice Hockey Skate Size	Inline Hockey Skate Size
	Ice Hockey Skate Size	Inline Hockey Skate Size	Ice Hockey Skate Size	Inline Hockey Skate Size
Y11	Y10	Y10	Y11	Y11
Y12	Y11	Y11	Y12	Y12
Y13	Y12	Y12	Y13	Y13
1	Y13	Y13	1	1
1.5	Y13	Y13	1.5	1.5
2	1	1	2	2
2.5	1	1	2.5	2.5
3	1.5	1.5	3	3
3.5	2	2	3.5	3.5
4	2.5	2.5	4	4
4.5	3	3	4.5	4.5
5	3.5	3.5	5	5
5.5	4	4	5.5	5.5
6.0	4.5	4.5	6	6
6.5	5	5	6.5	6.5
7	5.5	5.5	7	7
7.5	6	6	7.5	7.5
8	6.5	6.5	8	8
8.5	7	7	8.5	8.5
9	7.5	7.5	9	9
9.5	8	8	9.5	9.5
10	8.5	8.5	10	10
10.5	9	9	10.5	10.5

HELMETS, KEEP YOUR HEAD IN THE GAME!

Today's hockey helmets are designed to protect players from the many hazards that hockey delivers. It's hard to believe that just a few short years ago many hockey players played the game without a helmet! With pucks being shot at over 100 miles per hour, sharp skate blades, high sticks and thunderous body checks being delivered all over the ice, it is a miracle that we don't deal with more serious injuries on a regular basis. This should impress the importance of a good quality, new helmet. It's important to wear a good hockey helmet with sufficient padding to ward off concussion injuries. Experts recommend that it be at least 5/8 in thickness. Most helmets are made of a polycarbonate material, which is basically a light weight type of hard plastic. Hockey helmets come in one and two piece models, with the two piece version allowing a much more customized fit.

Your helmet should fit snug but not uncomfortable on all areas of your head. Your helmet should not move around on your head. If it does, it will reduce the protection ability and increase your chances of receiving a concussion. Your chinstrap should touch your chin with your mouth closed. You will need to adjust your helmet so it is snug without pinching anywhere on your head. Depending on the shape and size of your head, some helmets will just feel better than others. The helmet should fit flat on your head with about ½ an inch above the eyebrows, without it tilting forwards or back. Always make sure that your helmet doesn't shift around on your head during use.

HELMET SIZING CHART

Helmet Size	Hat Size	Circumference	Helmet Size	Hat Size	Circumference
Extra Small	6 3/8 - 6 7/8	20.0" - 21.5"	Extra Small	6 3/8 - 6 7/8	20.0" - 21.5"
Small	6 3/4 - 7 1/8	21.0" - 22.5"	Small	6 3/8 - 7	20" - 22"
Medium	7 - 7 1/2	22.0" - 23.5"	Medium	6 7/8 - 7 3/8	21.5" - 23"
Large	7 3/8 - 7 7/8	23.0" - 25.0"	Large	7 1/4 - 7 7/8	22.8" - 25"
Extra Large	7 3/4 - 8 1/4	24.5" - 26.0"	Extra Large	7 5/8 - 8 1/8	24" - 25.6"

A $20 MOUTH GUARD

This item may be the most underrated piece of equipment that you could purchase. Have you ever seen hockey player smile? There is usually a common theme, a lack of teeth. This should not come as a surprise. In today's game a 6-ounce hockey puck can reach speeds in excess of 100mph and can hit teeth with a force of over 1,250 ft/pounds.

Mouth guards are becoming mandatory in most Canadian hockey leagues, even if you are currently wearing a mask. Mouth guards not only protect your teeth, but they also soften any blow to the head. A mouth guard can not only help prevent concussions, but it also can help prevent cerebral hemorrhages, incidents of unconsciousness, jaw fractures and neck injuries. So, you can see the value; make your child wear a mouth guard at an early age. It is much easier to get used to playing with one before you get used to playing without one.

HOCKEY PANTS

Your hockey pants protect your midsection to the top of your shin pads. Above the waist, the pants should extend up to the lower end of the rib cage and the bottom of your shoulder pads. At the knee, your pants should overlap the top of your shin pads by one or two inches to provide coverage even when you bend your knees. Your pants should fit loose enough to allow for full range of motion in your waist and hips, but not so loose that they shift out of position. Most pants come with a belt so you can secure the pants at your waist. For most players, your waist size can be used to select your hockey pants.

HOCKEY DEVELOPMENT CAMPS

PANT SIZING CHART

Senior Sizing				
Size	Waist Size	Height	Weight (lbs)	Age
Small	30" - 34"	5'5" - 5'9"	120 - 160	14 +
Medium	32" - 36"	5'7" - 5'11"	140 - 180	14 +
Large	34" - 38"	5'9" - 6'1"	160 - 200	15 +
X-Large	36" - 40"	5'11" - 6'3"	180 - 220	15 +
XX-Large	40+	6'1" +	200 +	15 +
Junior Sizing				
Size	Waist Size	Height	Weight (lbs)	Age
Small	22" - 24"	4'3" - 4'7"	60 - 80	8 - 10
Medium	24" - 26"	4'6" - 4'10"	70 - 90	9 - 11
Large	26" - 28"	4'9" - 5'1"	85 - 100	10 - 12
Large Tall	26" - 28"	5'0" - 5'4"	85 - 100	10 - 12
X-Large	28" - 30"	5'0" - 5'4"	90 - 120	12 - 15

Elbow pads and gloves should provide continuous protection from above the elbow to the tips of your fingers. The cuff of the glove should extend to the bottom of your elbow pads leaving no part of your lower arm exposed. To protect your fingertips, your fingers should not go all the way to the end of the glove. Put on your elbow pads. Hold your arm and hand outstretched. Measure the distance between the tips of your fingers and the bottom of your elbow pad. If you prefer a shorter cuff, you may consider wearing protective wrist guards in the uncovered area.

HOCKEY DEVELOPMENT CAMPS

SHIN GUARDS

Shin guards are designed to protect the shins and knees from impacts that might occur from sticks, pucks, or other players. To determine the size of shin guard to order, you will need to measure the length of the shin. To do this you will need to bend the leg at a 90 degree angle. Then, measure from the center of the kneecap to the top of the boot of the skate. Make sure to measure all the way to the top of the boot, not to the top of the tongue of the skate. This will give you a measurement that will help to determine the proper shin guard size.

THE SHIN GUARDS ARE BEST MEASURED WHILE THE ATHLETE IS SITTING DOWN

Senior Sizing

Size	Age	Height	Weight (lbs)	Length
Small 13"	14 - +	5'5" - 5'9"	120 - 160	12 - 13
Medium 14"	14 - +	5'7" - 5'11"	140 - 180	13 - 14
Large 15"	15 - +	5'9" - 6'1"	160 - 200	14 - 15
X-Large 16"	15 - +	5'11" - 6'3"	180 - 220	15 - 16
XX-Large 17"	15 - +	6'1" - +	200 - +	16 - 17
XXX-Large 18"	15 - +	6'1" - +	200 - +	17 - 18

Junior Sizing

Size	Age	Height	Weight (lbs)	Length
Small 10"	8 - 11	4'3" - 4'8"	60 - 90	9 - 11
Medium 11"	9 - 12	4'7" - 5'	70 - 100	10 - 11
Large 12"	11 - 14	4'11" - 5'4"	80 - 110	10 - 12

Youth Sizing

Size	Age	Height	Weight (lbs)	Length
Small 7"	4 - 7	3'3" - 4'1"	40 - 60	6 - 7
Medium 8"	5- 8	3'7" - 4'4"	45 - 65	7 - 8

HOCKEY DEVELOPMENT CAMPS

ELBOW PADS

Your elbow pads protect your arm from the bicep extension of your shoulder pads to the cuff of your gloves leaving no part of your arm exposed. Your elbow should fit comfortably into the elbow pad cup and the elbow pad should fit securely without twisting or sliding on your arm. Your elbows are very susceptible to injury so make sure the pads fit securely and do not move around during play.

ELBOW PADS				
Senior Sizing				
Size	Age	Height	Weight (lbs)	Length
Small	14 - +	5'5" - 5'9"	120 - 160	12 - 13
Medium	14 - +	5'7" - 5'11"	140 - 180	13 - 14
Large	15 - +	5'9" - 6'1"	160 - 200	14 - 15
Junior Sizing				
Size	Age	Height	Weight (lbs)	Length
Small	8 - 11	4'3" - 4'10"	60 - 90	9 - 11
Large	11 - 14	4'7" - 5'4"	80 - 110	10 - 12
Youth Sizing				
Size	Age	Height	Weight (lbs)	Length
Small	4 - 7	3'3" - 4'1"	40 - 60	7 - 8
Large	6 - 9	3'9" - 4'7"	50 - 70	8 - 9

SHOULDER PADS

Shoulder pads are designed to protect the upper body including the upper arm, shoulder, collarbone, back, chest and ribs. You should choose a shoulder pad that offers the most padding in the chest area without inhibiting movement. To determine the size of shoulder pad to order, you will need to measure the circumference of the chest by placing a tape measure around the chest just under the armpits. This will give you a starting point for proper sizing.

HOCKEY DEVELOPMENT CAMPS

www.designerhockeydrills.com

Shoulder Pad Sizing Chart				
Senior Sizing				
Size	Age	Height	Weight (lbs)	Chest
Small	14 - +	5'5" - 5'9"	120 - 160	36 - 40
Medium	14 - +	5'7" - 5'11"	140 - 180	32 - 42
Large	15 - +	5'9" - 6'1"	160 - 200	40 - 44
X-Large	15 - +	5'11" - 6'3"	180 - 220	42 - +
Junior Sizing				
Size	Age	Height	Weight (lbs)	Chest
Small	8 - 11	4'3" - 4'8"	60 - 90	26 - 30
Medium	9 - 12	4'7" - 5'	70 - 100	28 - 32
Large	11 - 14	4'11" - 5'4"	80 - 110	30 - 34
Youth Sizing				
Size	Age	Height	Weight (lbs)	Chest
Small	4 - 7	3'3" - 4'1"	40 - 60	22 - 26
Large	6 - 9	3'9" - 4'7"	50 - 70	24 - 28

STICKS

Composite hockey sticks are now very complex and made for the expert player. With the Hockey Academy, I was able to spend some time using different types of composite sticks the players were using. I would borrow a new twig every week to try. The composite sticks are lighter and some give you a better feel for the puck but for the beginner, they are not necessary. These high priced sticks are like a golf club, they have a sweet spot and if you are not hitting the sweet spot you tend to lose accuracy and velocity. When you hit the sweet spot on a regular basis, these sticks can be lethal. For the beginner, save your money and buy the less expensive wood sticks. The wood sticks come in various cool colors and styles at a much more reasonable price.

The appearance is very important to the young player, no matter how it functions. If you want to test the waters with high priced sticks, my opinion is to go to a 2-piece stick. Your young athlete will go through several different sticks in his lifetime and a two-piece stick will allow you to change blades with different curves until your son or daughter finds that perfect fit.

After learning these few concepts about outfitting your child in the most knowledgeable way, you can now go with confidence to your local sport store, make informed decisions, stay within your budget and help your child have a successful year.

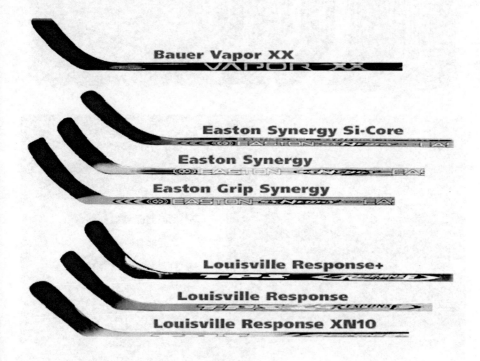

CHAPTER 2
REP VS. HOUSE, YOUR CHILD'S FIRST TRYOUT

The main decision that you and your child will make each year is whether or not to try out for the Travel or Rep team. This decision is usually based on the commitment level that the player and the parent are willing to make, plus the ability of the individual. If you love the game but have other interests, like school sports, and you don't want to commit to hockey in a full time basis, you probably should look at the house level. But if you love the game and have the dream and desire to play someday in the NHL, then great, make that commitment and go for it.

There will always be tryouts in hockey and they are going to be a very emotional and exciting time for both the parents and the player, just don't forget that it is also a very difficult time for the coaching staff. Coaches do not like "cutting" or letting players go to as it is always perceived as a negative, and they don't want the child to be hurt, but it must be done.

Being released to another team is not always a negative situation. Players that are on the bubble making a Rep team may have a better year and be one of the better players on the lower level team. They may get more ice time and play in many more important situations playing at a more suitable level. This will ultimately be a much more positive experience. Take being released as a challenge! Go to your new team and try to work your way back onto the team you originally tried out for. Prove that the coach was wrong for cutting you! Don't feel sorry for yourself, and never lose sight of your dream. Remember this, every player that has played in the NHL has been released from a team at one time or another during their career and many of them have been released several times. Where would they be if they just went out and quit. The good ones don't quit. They simply learn from their experiences and move on.

Disappointment aside, as parents you must consider several things when reacting or over reacting to any decision made by the coaching staff of the team your child is trying out for. Number one is the attitude of your child and how they react to being released. Your child must be first and foremost in your mind. Don't overreact. Listen to their thoughts and feelings. Do not get them more upset by telling him *"YOU SHOULD HAVE MADE THE TEAM, THE COACH IS AN IDIOT."* These comments always seem to be the right things to say when justifying your child's disappointment by not making that particular team. Too many parents also make a poor decision by telling everyone that they see that their son or daughter was not dealt with fairly. This becomes a vicious circle, and trust me, it will come back to haunt the player in the future. All you can do is provide your child with every opportunity to be successful, and if they are not successful in the tryout, support them in a positive way. Turn a negative into a positive. Have your son or daughter go and thank the coach for the opportunity for the tryout. Be sincere! Trust me. This will be a much better way to handle the situation. The coach that just released you will think to himself (WHAT A GREAT KID) and if the team ever has any injuries, guess who he will be most likely looking for? The player that acted like a mature young adult when they were released and parents that didn't interfere or the upset parents that made a scene when his son was let go. I know that as a coach myself, all coaches are looking for the hard working player and parents that can handle these situations in a professional manner.

HOCKEY DEVELOPMENT CAMPS

As a player, during your tryout, there are a couple of things you can control. *WORK ETHIC AND ATTITUDE.* Coaches are always looking for these qualities in any athlete. If you really want to make the team, don't be lazy at any time on the ice. Keep your feet moving and never give up. Give the coaches your very best and it will make it difficult for them to release you. Be aggressive and show no fear from any other players. If you can play with this kind of passion, any coach will need to have a second look at you no matter what your skill level.

Mistakes are a big part of the game, how you react to them is another way to get noticed in a positive or negative matter. If you go into camp with the mindset that, I CANT MAKE ANY MISTAKES OR I WILL NOT MAKE THE TEAM, you will not play at your best. If you play the game with the fear of making a mistake you will play very apprehensively and you will just fade in with all the rest of the players. What you need to do is to stick out. Be the guy that the coaches are talking about. You want the coaches to notice you. There are far too many players that think they have had a great camp by not making any glaring errors on the ice, to find out that they are still released. Coaches are looking for players that are confident and not afraid of making mistakes, and when you do make a mistake (trust me you will), be accountable. If you are a defenseman and you get beat, and the other team scores, don't drop your head and run off the ice. Go down and give your goalie a pat, tell him that this was your fault and it won't happen again. Any coach that sees that kind of maturity will remember you. Camps are very short and the coaches and evaluators only get a small window of time before they need to make difficult decisions, so do not take a shift off as it could be the one that the coaches are watching you.

If you are put on a line with weaker players again do not take it negatively. Make it a challenge! Go out and be the leader on that line and show that you are a leader yourself. It is all the little things that you do on and off the ice that will help you make these teams.

In the dressing room, be a quality individual. Do not get into any of the name calling, making fun of other players or any other of the things that go on in most dressing rooms. You do not have to be the best friend of all your teammates, but you must be able to respect your teammates both on and off the ice.

HOCKEY DEVELOPMENT CAMPS

As a potential player for any team, coaches will also be looking for chemistry. Make sure you are polite to all the players' whether you like them or not and no matter what their skill level may be.

During minor hockey tryouts there will be several types of players. The ones that are there with hopes of making the team, the ones that feel they are already on the team, and players that are at the tryouts just for the experience and looking for extra ice time.

Parents, as your child goes through the tryout process, make sure you are simply there to watch, be positive, and enjoy the hockey. The worst thing a parent can do is to be too involved. Usually during any tryout, the coaching staff and the evaluators will have a meeting and let the players and parents know what to expect during this process. You simply are a bystander. Also, remember the coach could be a friend of yours and also have a son trying out for the team.

Always remember that the coach is there to pick the best players to make the best team possible for the upcoming season, they are not there strictly to pick on your son or daughter. The Coach has gone through an interview process to get this position and the minor hockey organization thinks he is the most qualified person to run that team. The Coach will no doubt make some decisions that are unpopular to the players and parents. This is just the nature of hockey tryouts, and you need to respect it. As a parent at any level of hockey, you do not want to be known as a parent that can't accept decisions made by the coach. You will make it more difficult for your child to have any success during tryouts.

After the team is picked, every coach wants to have the support of the parents, as well as the players. This is the main ingredient of a highly competitive and hard working team. By being supportive it helps create a fun environment for the kids to play in. If your child is released during any camp, be positive with him and go to the next level team and have a great season with no regrets. You may not agree with the decision, but it will not change by becoming an irate irrational parent, the type that no one wants to be around, because there are already too many of them.

CHAPTER 3
PARENTS' AND PLAYERS' RELATIONSHIP WITH THE COACH

Coaches in every organization usually go through a very specific interview process to determine whether he or she is the right person for the team. Usually in larger organizations, there are several applicants for each position, and yes there is usually a parent or two that has put his name in the ring to coach. In almost all the organizations that I interviewed, they would like a non parent coach at the rep level, if possible. These coaches are volunteers, but the team pays their expenses. Coaches, parents and players have always had a love hate relationship. Being a coach on a rep team or any team for that matter, it is difficult to make all the players happy with their ice time or their leadership roles. In this Chapter you will have a better understanding of what the coaches go through, how the players react to the coaches and how the reaction of the parents can affect the player, the coach and the team as a whole.

First, let's discuss the role and expectations of the coach. The coach must have been successful in the selection process and hopefully now has the organization on his side. The head coaches' responsibility is to recruit a coaching staff that will help him with the details within the team. He will need a Team Manager to help with the organization of tournaments, collecting fees for the coaches and any team expenses. The Manager also helps with finding exhibition games. Usually in minor hockey it is a parent off the team that is recruited to take on this task. It is very wise for the coach to not worry about this position until the team is selected as it will undoubtedly lead to speculation that the player of the team manager was already selected to the team before the tryouts have even started. It is also not a good idea for any parent to accept a position within a rep team until the team is selected. Head Coaches do have the authority to obtain their own assistant coaches, however the assistants usually need to be approved by the association.

The first duty of the coach during tryouts should be to meet with the players and parents to let them know how the tryout process will be executed. For parents this the time to speak up and ask any questions about the team and the selection process. If you are confused about any details of the camp get the proper information explained to you before your Childs first ice session.
Once the camp starts you, as a parent, must now be a supportive spectator. Every team has several types of parents, and they all must be able to co-exist during the year. Parent type one: Is very competitive and wants to win. They will be in favor of any extra ice time and all the tournaments the team can play in. A really hands on parent. This parent also will be the one that is usually the most vocal, typically in regards to officiating. They are usually the parent of one of the better players on the team. Their child is getting most of the ice time and is a very important part of the team's success. It is ok to be proud of your player and involved to a certain extent, but be aware of how your involvement is affecting your son or Daughter and the team as a whole.

The next parent type is the one that quietly supports the team doesn't get to involved with any part of the team. They are supportive but not so interested in spending a lot of money on their player's year. They just listen in the stands and are usually appalled about what is being said about the officiating, coaches, and players on the team. This parent just wants his child to have a great experience and enjoy the game, unfortunately that parent usually goes home shaking their heads, wondering what they have gotten themselves into. This is obviously a conflict that can escalate into problems between parents and players alike. Parents in the stands, remember this key term (**FHR**). *Friendship*. Your player is friends with several players on the team, if not all of them, so don't get involved with any putdowns of players, their play etc, as you never know when it is going to come back and bite you in the butt. *Harassment*. Keep in mind that anything you say in the stands that is negative or hurtful in context is considered harassment. It never seems to be dealt with by the law, but is sure enforced by the parent of the player you are talking about no matter which team they are playing for. There have been several major altercations that resulted from bantering in the stands. Remember you are supposed to be setting an example for these young players. *Role model*. Remember that whatever you do or however you react to any situation at the rink, you child is watching you. You as a parent are the biggest influence in your child's life so if you can't control your emotions during a simple hockey game, you can expect your child to act the same way. Remember, you are always being watched.

The main concept to have a successful team that not many people or players understand is; **you are only as strong as your weakest player**. This concept is not the problem; it is how people react to this situation. I always tell my players that you have two choices to make to being a good teammate. Number one, you can choose to isolate those weaker players and not make them part of the team, ridicule them and have them not enjoy the hockey experience and probably not play up to their potential. Or number two, the right way, bring in any struggling teammates, make them feel important and help them in any way possible. Support them and I guarantee that throughout the course of the year, these teammates will do everything they can to improve as players and help the team.

Even NHL players are faced with the same decisions. Stars like Joe Sakic, Steve Yzerman, Jarome Iginla, Mark Messier, and Sidney Crosby have, several times throughout their career, taken struggling players under their wing to help them achieve success. They did this to help the team succeed because they were true leaders.

The 24-hour rule. This has been around minor sports for a long time. The rule is simply this; if you or your player has experienced something that is bothersome or disruptive to themselves during a game or practice, take 24 hours before reporting it to the coach or team representative. This is just a cooling off period where a lot of the time the problem is not as big as once thought. Before bringing it to your coaches attention think clearly about how it may affect your player, in either a positive or negative way. Be sure you are doing the right thing, not just lashing out because you are upset about your player's ice time, the position they are playing or anything regarding your fellow parents or teammates.

The Dreaded Drive Home. Hockey is a very subjective sport. You may think that the team played very well, whereas the coach thinks the team stunk. It is fine to have a different opinion but do not get your player all riled up on the way home trying to instill your own coaching beliefs on your player. Always try to turn a negative into a positive. You might react by saying the coach sure thinks you are going to be a very good team, because in the stands we thought the team played not that bad. Just think of the success your team is going to have when you start to play your very best hockey. You guys could win a lot of games. Even if you don't think the coach is right, remember that you are there for the entire season. Make it a positive one for you, your family and your player. Do not coach your son or daughter on the way home. Support your coach and if you must, add to the concepts he is trying to get across to his team. Every team system will work if all the players and parents buy into the concept.

HOCKEY DEVELOPMENT CAMPS

Hockey Story. The score was tied late in the second period. Both teams were skating at a grueling pace and checking more fiercely than you'd imagine pre-teens would or could. This was the best hockey we have seen in years featuring 10 of the best teams of 11-year-olds in British Columbia. The loser of this game would be eliminated from the tournament. Suddenly, one of the players picked up the puck at the red line, fought off a check and angled himself to the net. He flashed across the goal mouth and backhanded a shot that passed over the goalie's shoulder, but just deflected off the post. No goal. "His old man is going to kill him," said Karson, whose son Cameron was on the team. Standing three rows below him, another father, Graham, whose son Gerry was a defenseman also on the team, turned around and said. "And rightfully so," Were they kidding? Well, they weren't being literal, of course.

But if you travel for the weekend with any competitive hockey team, what you see - aside from some exciting hockey - are parents on a balance beam, intent on supporting their children but always in danger of slipping off into self-interest and allowing their children's dreams to become their own. Understandable as it is that they are excited by their sons' skills and triumphs, many of any teams' parents openly admit that the excitement of the game could skew their judgment and that they struggled with the line between serious support of your hockey player and going overboard.

Not until I lived this story did I realize the magnitude of how serious parents take this game. Only after interviewing several of these parents did they actually understand that what they were doing could be perceived as such a negative influence. They were just caught up in the game and didn't realize that what they were doing was wrong on so many levels. Next time you go to the rink just listen to the parents conversations. Unfortunately this happens in every rink across North America. But it doesn't have to.

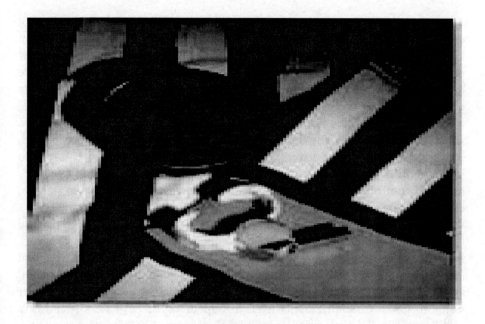

CHAPTER 4
RESPECT FOR THE OFFICIALS

This has got to be the most disturbing area of Today's Hockey Industry. We continually criticize the Officials in every sport and at every age level. Hockey, as all sports need some sort of discipline, people to enforce the rules and integrity of the game. What we don't seem to understand is these officials just like the players are also learning the game, especially at the minor hockey levels. It is not uncommon to see a Bantam rep game, with 13, 14 year olds, having their referee being only a couple of years older than the players themselves, plus the linesmen being the exact same age as the players involved in the game. What these young impressionable officials go through is at times boarder line criminal. They take abuse from everyone in the rink, they are constantly ridiculed as every game has two teams, and every call is going to have a positive and negative review for each call made on the ice, In short really, the officials can never win.

Parents have got to be the worst critics of the game, and they are not even playing the game, or involved in any way, so why do we as parents get involved in the games our children play in. The answer is simple. We as parents are totally blind when it comes to common sense and athletics. We are much more competitive than the kids in the game. Maybe we react as parents because we unlike the players have a place to release our frustration; it builds within our competitive souls, and usually comes out in the most negative ways. Calling the officials down, the other teams players down, getting into confrontation with other parents from other teams. All in all, we turn into immoral, irrational ranting parents. It is not all the parents that don't seem to have self control, but it only takes one or two unreasonable parents to ruin the experience for all involved.

The sporting industry is constantly looking for young people to partake in officiating clinics and getting these young officials doing games at a very early age. The problem is that a lot of work goes into training officials, and then they run into those idiotic parents that can't keep their big mouths shut, and that young official is intimidated to the point that he or she no longer wants to be an official. Parents need to remember this. All the officials are usually young and very impressionable; they are not here to hurt your son, your team, or the integrity of the game. Officials are trained to enforce the rules, without the use of video replay. So yes the officials are going to make unpopular calls and they are also going to make mistakes, but we as parents must be able to take the good with the bad, they are part of the game. All officials are making subjective decisions so you are going to get referee's that call the game tight, and you will get officials that will let the kids play trying to just enforce the obvious infractions. You will run into each type of official at every level of the game, so get used to it, let the kids play and keep your opinions to yourself. Unless you have actually been an official, you have no idea how hard it is to referee a game.

Parents have blinders on when it comes to officiating a game with their child in it. Next time you go to the rink before your son plays his game, their usually will be a game playing, go into the stands and sit with the parents, from one of the teams. This is what you will hear; those parents bitching about missed calls, maybe a goal that was disallowed, or an offside. The problem with this is that every one of the complaints is about the other team.

You will very seldom hear that "wow, we got away with that one", and if it is said, it will be said in such a quiet manner that it will be hard for anyone to hear. But if the infraction happens to their team, they scream bloody murder; they yell at the ref, say all the mature things like "you need glasses", etc. I think if you have a serious look at how other fans act, you may be appalled and understand just how foolish you actually look!

Players are no different when it comes to officials. They have very little respect for the officials, which is an area that all players need to be much better at. I tell my players before every game, we have two choices when it comes to reacting to official's decisions. Number one is to act immature, argue the call, make the official remember you and your attitude, slap your stick on the ice, and basically make an ass of yourself. Or you can take the road that may help you later on in the game, just go to the box and focus on what you are going to do when you return to the ice. Don't let your emotions get the best of you, even if it was a bad call. As in all my years of hockey, I have never seen an official change his mind because a player or coach objected the call.

Players must be able to work the referee to his advantage, being professional respectful and direct to the officials will believe it or not, help you to possibly get a call go your way late in the game.

I know that officials are supposed to be impartial and just call the game as they see it. This is the way the officials are taught, but it may not always happen that way. I interviewed over 100 officials at various minor hockey levels and ask the direct question. If you notice a player on the ice, being disrespectful to his officiating staff or had a personal confrontation with a player, would you be more incline to look for that player again to give him another penalty, even the slightest infraction?

No official would come out and say "yeah, I would like to put that player in his place". But they all indicated that the individual would be watched a little more carefully during the game. Something you definitely don't need. Also if a player continually abuses an official, he is quickly labeled as a High Risk player, a label you do not want. So no matter how intense the game, and how bad the officiating is perceived, as a player, keep your cool and just play the game; you and your team will be better for it. Let the coaches' deal with the officiating- that is what they are there for.

CHAPTER 5
HOCKEY SCHOOLS, SHOULD YOU GO, WHERE TO GO TO, AND WHY?

Hockey schools are a multi-million dollar business with the primary focus on making money, then the development of the player. Is this wrong? Of course not. These schools are businesses first; hockey training facilities second. The number one topic in all hockey schools is Power Skating. With the rule changes in today's game, skating is even more important to every player. Gone are the days when a big, strong player could get by with average skating skills. With holding and interference being called more than ever, the game is much more in favor of the offensive players with great skating skills. The difficult task for all hockey schools is to focus on skating while making the experience enjoyable for the player, as all schools want you to return the next year.

In today's game we see several hockey players quitting the game at an early age because of HOCKEY BURNOUT, this term is not used very often but it should be. Parents and players still feel that they need to play the game all year around, with spring league teams and summer hockey schools available to all that can afford it.

ALL HOCKEY SCHOOLS ARE GOOD FOR YOUR PLAYER. The questions you need to answer are: What kind of budget do you have? Do you want to make a family holiday out of it? Is your player old enough to go on their own? How long are you going to go for? Are any of his friends going at the same time? Looking around North America, there are hundreds of hockey schools that come up on the internet. They all offer the same fundamental skating, shooting, checking and stick handling drills. They all seem to offer some sort of lectures, and a specific dry land program with a report card at the end of the week. The duration of the programs vary from 3-7 consecutive days. The one constant within all the schools is that they offer all this information using qualified instructors, in a safe and positive environment. Just remember going to a hockey school every year is not going to be the determining factor whether your son is going to play in the NHL.

The main selling point to almost all of these hockey schools is the instruction. Now, be careful with the information on the brochure. A lot of schools have top name former NHL players named as there instructors and of course the brochure is correct, to a point. The question is how often will your player be actually taught the skills by these NHL players? The answer is very little. This is not a bad thing; it is just something you should be aware of in your school selection. Every school will have an average of 25-40 skaters on the ice at one time. And the key will be the ratio of instructors per player. In most cases, the best scenario is a 4 or 5 player to one instructor ratio. This means that on the ice at any one time there will be up to 8 instructors, and trust me they will not all be former NHL players, in fact some of them might just be good minor hockey players. They will still do a good job as the program is set out by the professionals and they are just administering the program under the supervision of a head instructor, probably the pro we spoke about earlier.

This is not always the case. I was fortunate enough to be able to work with the largest and longest running hockey school in the world for several years. This school was the most detailed oriented school that I have ever gone to or seen. The Hockey School not only sold the head instructors as being former NHL players, but they also utilized them in all their programs. The NHL players worked as many hours as anyone else, if not more. Hockey Schools are programs, simple as that. If they are done well, most people can run a very good hockey school.

The one element that you need to consider is who will be running the power skating part of the program? Not the flashiest part of the program, but definitely the most important part. Having a certified Power Skating instructor will make sure that you are getting proper instruction in the most critical area, and usually the power skating instructor is not a NHL player. You need someone to be able to break down and teach the skills, not just be able to do the skills. So find out who is going to be the power skating instructor before registering.

Your next thought should be the supervision of your child during the transition from each facility. If it is a day camp, do they have counselors and are they with the kids at all times? The last thing you need to make sure of is your child. Are they motivated to go and want to go? Not you, the parent, thinking they will be better next year if they go. Remember, it must be your player wanting to improve and put in the effort to do so. Hockey schools are meant to allow your child to be in a healthy environment where you can try new ideas and not be scolded for making mistakes.

If you want to be a complete hockey player. ALWAYS ATTACK YOUR WEAKNESSES FIRST. This simply means work on the things that you are not great at or comfortable with. Maybe you turn to the left with ease. In practice, turn to the right as much as you can. Everyone has a favorite side to stop, so attack your weak side. Continue to identify your weaknesses and continue to try to improve them. Hockey schools are a great environment to challenge you. Alternatively, you may have the choice to play on a spring league team. These teams usually pick the better players and it is run like a rep team so be aware of the intentions of the coaches. Spring leagues here in Canada are fast becoming a huge success, with teams available in almost every center. If you love the game and can afford it, maybe spring league is for you.

Another alternative is to simply take the summer off, play soccer, baseball, basketball, lacrosse or any other sport that you may be interested in. Cross training is also a very good way to get ready for the upcoming hockey season. There is no rule that says that you must play hockey all year around. So let your player make the decision which direction they want ,remember that less than ½ of a percent of today's hockey players make a living at it, so the main objective is to raise a healthy, happy and well adjusted child.

CHAPTER 6
THE CANADIAN HOCKEY LEAGUES BANTAM DRAFT

The Bantam Draft for young Canadian hockey players is always of importance to kids, only because of the hype behind it. The Bantam Draft is a chance for the CHL Clubs to protect some of the young so called budding stars. In fact the Bantam draft is not nearly as important to players once you understand how it works.

Each CHL Club is allowed to add up to 50 players between the ages of 14 and 20 onto its Protected Player List (PPL). 14-year-olds may not be added to the list until the Bantam Draft has been completed following their second year at the bantam level. The 50 Player Protected List is used by the Western Hockey League, the Ontario Hockey League and the Quebec Major Junior league.

This is to ensure there is a method of organization and control in the League for the rights to players. The system would be problematic, without this type of built in control.

All players on a WHL Club's roster are required to be on the 50 Player Protected List, so if a WHL Club is carrying 23 players, this leaves only 27 spots available for future prospects. Needless to say, only the elite players will be represented on a Club's List. If a player on the List no longer meets the expectations of the team, he will be replaced by another prospect. As a result, the List is constantly changing as teams evaluate their players and make adjustments. Clubs are permitted to make changes to their 50 Player List throughout the entire year.

Competing with the NCAA

The Canadian Hockey League provides the top young hockey talent in North America with the opportunity to develop their skills on the ice at the highest possible level, without compromising their academic goals.
Each CHL Club has an Education Advisor that tracks the academic progress of all players throughout the season. While playing in the CHL, players receive financial assistance for education expenses such as high school tutoring or fees for post-secondary courses, to ensure players reach their academic potential. While a player's primary on-ice goal is to win the League Championship and compete for the storied Memorial Cup, it is equally important for that player to set his sights on academic success as well. CHL Club's are governed by League-wide Education Standards that ensure players complete their high school in timely fashion and achieve the highest level of academic success possible.

The CHL is committed to recognizing academic excellence. Awards are presented annually to each league's academic Scholastic Player and Scholastic Team of the Year. The Canadian Hockey League is recognized as the best and quickest way to progress the NHL. The CHL started this education process as they were continually losing potential players to NCAA scholarships, through Junior A hockey in Canada. This process in the CHL is a very good system for the right player. The CHL awards 1 year of education for each year played. The only problem with this is that if you go to play in the CHL, and get released, your so called education is only paid for each full year you actually complete, plus you have lost your eligibility to receive a NCAA athletic Scholarship.

So at a young age, you must be careful and well educated in making these difficult decisions. It is imperative for a CHL Club to build their List with quality players if they wish to be competitive in the future. By limiting each Club's List to 50 players, this ensures that the talent level will be consistent throughout the CHL, while still rewarding the Clubs who do the best job in scouting talent. With only 50 available spots, this means that decisions must be made carefully to ensure the Club's future viability. Although many players are added to CHL Club Lists during the Bantam Draft, there are also numerous situations where players develop later and are listed at that time. The following NHL stars were not selected in the CHL Bantam Draft but were added to a CHL Club's list at a later date: Jerome Iginla, Darcy Tucker, Jeff Friesen, Dan Hamhuis, Scottie Upshall, Joffrey Lupul, Jeff Woywitka, and Shane Doan.

A player who is on a CHL Club's List may not play for another CHL team, or attend another CHL Club's training camp or rookie camp. However, being a member of a CHL team's 50 Player Protected List does not restrict a player from playing for, or attending a camp of a non-CHL Club. The 50 Player Protected List is used strictly to determine which CHL team holds the player's rights.

The WHL, along with the Ontario Hockey League and the Quebec Major Junior Hockey League comprise the Canadian Hockey League. Rules are in place to ensure that a player may be selected by only one League.

As you can see, the Bantam draft is not so important. For players that are drafted, sure it is a great honor, but you are still 2 years away from even being able to suit up for that team. Plus, you need to be aware of your eligibility for possible college scholarships down the road, and how much time you can spend with the CHL team during training camp before you jeopardize your academic eligibility. For example, if you are at a training camp over 48 hours you could lose 1 year of academic eligibility with regards to an NCAA scholarship. Again, as parents you must do the research and make sure you are keeping your child's options open. At the tender age of 14, 15 or 16 it is very difficult to decide to play in the CHL and you need to make sure you are making the right decision. It should not be influenced by a coach. It must be a family decision with all the current information in front of you. Then and only then should you sit down and decide the best path to take. It is never an easy decision, but it must be an educated one.

CHAPTER 7
SCHOOL AND ATHLETICS, YOUR KEY TO ACADEMIC SUCCESS

Hockey is one of the major sports in Canada that can offer your son or daughter an academic Scholarship for excelling in their chosen sport. This in mind, too many players don't do the little things throughout their minor hockey career to stay eligible to receive a scholarship. This is where you, the parent comes in. The NCAA allows each Division 1 ice hockey program 18 scholarships for men and 18 for women.

In high school, you should be aware that the standard of hockey at the college level is very high. I would recommend that you attend a few games to gauge the actual intensity and athletic ability of the hockey being played. Remember that only the absolute top hockey players will be approached by recruiting officers.

Athletes basically have 5 "College years" to complete 4 years of athletic eligibility Students who do not meet the minimum academic requirements or fail to register will almost certainly lose one of those years.

Parents, this is a great opportunity to help your player keep good grades in school. Colleges and universities today look at Academics all the way back to their first year in High School. Grades 9 through 12 are very important years for your student athlete. There is a multitude of information supporting these statements. You can make your child aware of these academic needs. The better the student, the better chance they have in landing a college Scholarship. Of course, they must also excel at the game as well, The 2 go hand in hand. Understanding this information, I know your child will take more interest in school if they think that they must do well academically in order to be eligible for a Hockey Scholarship.

It is your job to hold your player accountable, making sure to maintain the proper balance between academics and athletics. This information is a great tool to keep your player interested in school. Below is current information regarding athletics and the details and some suggestions regarding understanding and preparing your student athlete for the possibility of a Hockey Scholarship. Failing to prepare is preparing to fail. Stay educated and up to date.

Ivy League "Scholarships"

The first thing you need to know is that all scholarships awarded by the Ivy League are **"need based."** That means that the only students who receive Ivy League financial aid are those whose families cannot afford to pay full pop. However, even many students from "comfortable" middle-class homes receive some sort of scholarship assistance due to the high price tag attached to these schools.

The way Ivy League colleges operate is that they first evaluate their applicants based on their qualifications. In order to be eligible to consider applying to an Ivy League college you have to maintain tip-top grades (usually close to a straight-A average), with the vast majority of your classes selected from the toughest ones available to you. (Admission officials don't penalize you if your school doesn't offer any AP or even honors classes, but they do like it when you turn to a local community college or find other enrichment opportunities, if your own school isn't very challenging.)

Your SAT I and II scores are also very important, but these may be changing in the near future. These scores are probably more important than most admission folks are willing to admit. In fact, College Confidential offers an "Academic Index" calculator that is similar to the system that Ivies uses to compare candidates. You can read more about this at <u>Academic Index</u> but as a freshman you probably don't have test scores yet and won't be able to try it.

Finally, your essay(s), recommendations, and extracurricular activities are all evaluated from a more subjective standpoint (i.e. no formulas used here). Not surprisingly, the Ivy League schools receive stacks of applications from amazing students who excel in a wide range of areas. Typically, an Ivy applicant has to be more than just a good student with lots of extracurricular activities.

The Ivy League schools are looking for **student government** presidents and yearbook **editors-in-chief**. Moreover, they're also seeking students with unusual accomplishments—not just the same old, familiar high school stuff, however impressive it may be. Thus, applicants who have published books, danced on Broadway, or founded a national charity may get extra attention at decision time, even if their grades and SATs aren't quite up to snuff. (They still have to be good, of course.) Not surprisingly, recruited athletes also get special attention (and some slack) when it comes to transcripts and test scores. But don't count on it.

Applicants are never evaluated equally either. That is, admission officials pay close attention to such factors as background family dynamics and a range of other extenuating circumstances that a student has had to face.

Now, to get back to your original question … once admission officers have "graded" a student, they put together the final list of those they wish to admit. In most cases, each of these admitted students is then awarded what that college believes is enough financial aid to attend. For some students, this will be the entire cost of tuition, room and board, and perhaps even money for transportation and books. For others, it will be nothing. The strongest candidates don't get more financial aid than the more borderline ones. It's all based on family finances.

There are some variations to this system. For instance, a college that is not "need blind" will make some "fine tuning" decisions about candidates based on their ability to pay, but that doesn't happen until the very end of the evaluation process, and a very strong applicant—however poor—will most likely be admitted and receive a generous scholarship. Some colleges are "need blind" for U.S. citizens and permanent residents but not for international students.

Thus, the only way to win a scholarship from an Ivy League college is to get yourself admitted. This means being an exceptional student with an exceptional list of accomplishments as well. Even then, there is a certain element of luck involved. Many highly qualified candidates are turned away each year, often with no apparent reason. You also have to come from a family with "demonstrated need." Thus, the bad news: No matter how smart or talented you are, you will not get a scholarship from the Ivy League if your parents can afford to pay your way. The good news, however, is that–if admitted—you should not have to pass up an Ivy education for financial reasons, because the colleges promise to meet your monetary need, no matter how high.

National Collegiate Athletic Association (NCAA)
What is the NCAA?

The National Collegiate Athletic Association (NCAA) is a voluntary organization through which American colleges and universities govern their athletics programs. It comprises more than 1,250 institutions, conferences, organizations and individuals.

What do I need to do to compete in the NCAA?

In order to compete in the NCAA you must graduate from high school, write the SAT or ACT, register with the NCAA Clearinghouse, meet NCAA academic standards, remain academically and athletically eligible to compete and be admitted to an NCAA institution.

How many universities offer hockey programs?

There are approximately 58 Division I, and 74 Division III hockey programs.

Division I and III
What is Division I?

Division I is the highest level of athletic competition in the NCAA. Athletic programs at Division I universities can offer financial aid or scholarships based solely on athletic ability.

What is Division III?

Division III universities focus much more on the academic experience than on the athletic experience of the student-athlete. As such Division III universities prohibit financial aid or scholarships based on athletic ability only. Furthermore, rules and regulations governing competition in Division III athletics are less stringent than those that govern competition in Division I.

NCAA Initial Eligibility Clearinghouse
What is the NCAA Clearinghouse?

The NCAA Clearinghouse is an agency which performs amateurism certification and determines the NCAA academic eligibility of all student-athletes wishing to compete in NCAA Division I or II athletics (Note: Division III institutions individually determine the eligibility of their incoming student-athletes.)

The clearinghouse evaluates student courses, grades and test scores to determine whether students meet prescribed minimum academic requirements and will provide the student's initial-eligibility certification results to all universities that request this information. Any prospective student-athlete who will enroll in College and compete in NCAA Division I or Division II athletics must register with the Clearinghouse. Initial-eligibility certification from the clearinghouse does not guarantee your admission to any Division I or II college. You must apply for college admission separately. The clearinghouse only determines whether you meet NCAA requirements as a freshman student-athlete in a Division I or II college to be able to compete, practice and receive an athletic scholarship.

What is Amateurism Certification?

Amateurism certification is a process to determine the amateur status of freshman and transfer student athletes initially enrolling at NCAA Divisions I and II member institutions. Prospects will complete an amateurism section when they register with the NCAA Initial-Eligibility Clearinghouse. Amateurism certification will consider a student-athlete's:

- o Contracts with a professional team (Division I).
- o Salary for participating in athletics (Division I).
- o Prize money above actual and necessary expenses (Division I).
- o Play with professionals (Division I).
- o Tryouts, practice or competition with a professional team (Division I).
- o Benefits from an agent or prospective agent (Divisions I and II).
- o Agreement to be represented by an agent (Divisions I and II).
- o Organized-competition rule (Divisions I and II).

When should I register for the Clearinghouse?

If you wish to compete in the NCAA in the future you should register with the NCAA Clearinghouse after completion of grade 11, or as soon as possible thereafter, even if you have not received an offer to attend an NCAA university.

How do I register for the Clearinghouse?

1. Go to www.ncaaclearinghouse.net
2. Click on "*Prospective Student-Athletes*"
3. Click on "*Registration Form for Foreign Students*" found in the left-hand pane
4. Complete the form
5. Send required documents
- *Registration Form for Foreign Students*
- Registration fee
- High school transcripts
- Proof of high school graduation (most likely stated on transcripts)
- ACT or SAT score report sent directly to the clearinghouse

How do I send a score report to institutions that request one?

To have SAT, SAT II or ACT score sent directly to the Clearinghouse:

a. Enter code 9999 on the registration form or answer document to have scores sent directly to the NCAA Clearinghouse, or

b. Contact the test administrator to request a score report be sent to the NCAA

How do I contact the NCAA Clearinghouse?
Go to www.ncaaclearinghouse.net for contact information.

Athletic Scholarships
What are athletic scholarships?
Athletic scholarships are 1-year contracts officially called "National Letters of Intent." These contracts are between the university and the student-athlete and are awarded based on some degree on athletic ability.

What is a "National Letter of Intent"?
National Letter of Intent (NLI) is the official term for an "athletic scholarship" and is a binding agreement between a student-athlete and an institution in which the institution agrees to provide athletics aid for one academic year in exchange for the prospect's agreement to attend the institution for one academic year. All Colleges and Universities that participate in the NLI program agree to not recruit a prospective student-athlete once he/she signs an NLI with another college or university. Therefore, a prospective student-athlete who signs an NLI should no longer receive recruiting contacts and calls and is ensured an athletics' scholarship for one academic year. The NLI must be accompanied by an institutional financial aid agreement. If the student-athlete does not enroll at that institution for a full academic year, he/she may be subject to specific penalties, including loss of a season of eligibility and a mandatory residence requirement.

What is covered by an athletic scholarship?
Funds for tuition, books, room and board, and sometimes other expenses (i.e. travel to and from university from home).

Are scholarships guaranteed for 4-years?
There are no guaranteed 4-year athletic scholarships. All athletic scholarships are renewed on a year-by year basis. However, it is common for university athletic programs to make longer-term verbal commitments of 4 years. However, it is important to note that verbal commitments are not legally binding.

Who decides if I get a scholarship?

Although admissions offices can refuse the admission of any student thereby refusing any athletic scholarship, university athletic programs have considerable influence with the admission office. This allows coaches to scout and recruit players and offer scholarships to those who they want for their programs.

Does every student-athlete receive a 100% "full-scholarship"?

Typically, University hockey teams carry 22-26 players and have 18 "full-scholarships" to distribute at they see fit. Usually, of these 18 athletic scholarships some are divided into partial athletic scholarships and some remain full athletic scholarships. Most teams have some student-athletes who receive only a portion of their expenses in scholarship and some athletes who receive all their expenses in scholarship.

Can athletic scholarships be cancelled if I play bad or the coach doesn't like me?

If you are receiving an athletic scholarship, the scholarship may be reduced or canceled during the academic year only if you:

o Render yourself ineligible for NCAA competition; or

o Misrepresented any information on your application, letter of intent or financial aid agreement; or

o Commit serious misconduct which warrants a substantial disciplinary penalty; or

o Voluntarily quit the team for personal reasons.

Athletic scholarships may not be reduced, canceled or increased during the period of award:

o Based on your ability, performance, or contribution to your team's success; or

o Because an injury prevents you from participating; or

o For any other athletics reason.

Can I keep my scholarship if I am not playing on the team?

Because athletic scholarships are awarded for athletic participation, if you either quit the team or are released based on the grounds listed above you will lose your athletic scholarship.

How is an athletic scholarship renewed?

The decision to renew a scholarship is made on a year-by-year or term-by-term basis, depending on the regulations of the institution. If you are receiving an athletic scholarship, the institution must notify you in writing on or before July 1 whether the aid has been renewed or not renewed for the next academic year. This written notification comes from the institution's financial aid authority and not from the athletics department.

If the institution decides not to renew your athletic scholarship, or is going to reduce the amount of the scholarship, the institution must notify you in writing that you have the right to a hearing.

What universities offer athletic scholarships?

Athletes can receive athletic scholarships to Division I and II universities only. However, there are a number of universities within Division I that offer financial aid rather than athletic scholarships.

Financial Aid
What is financial aid?

Financial aid is a grant from the university that is not based on athletic ability or participation on a college or university team.

What is covered by financial aid?

Financial aid can be granted for tuition and fees, room and board, books and transportation.

How do universities determine "financial need" when that is the main criteria for receiving financial aid?

Although determining "financial need" varies between universities, it is typically calculated based on the student's savings and expected earnings over the summer, as well as the parents' overall wealth (earnings, savings, equity, investments etc).

The university makes a judgment on the amount that the student and parents are able to contribute towards a university education. Any shortfall between expected contribution and university expenses (tuition, room and board, books, and transportation) is covered by financial aid.

Can I keep my financial aid if I am not playing on the team?

Because non-athletic financial aid is not premised on athletic ability you will continue to receive financial aid if you are not on the hockey team. However, if you are released from the team for disciplinary reasons or for failing to meet academic standards the school may rescind future financial aid.

What universities offer financial aid?

Financial aid is offered at a variety of universities. Most Division III universities offer financial aid, as do many universities in Division I such as those in the Ivy League.

ACADEMIC ELIGIBILITY
Academic Eligibility

How many years of academic eligibility do I have to compete in NCAA athletics?

In general, student-athletes have 10 semesters (5 years) to complete the academic requirements of a university degree while playing NCAA athletics. If at any point you enroll full-time at a post-secondary institution in Canada or the US your "academic clock" (i.e. 5 years) begins to count down and can never be stopped. Therefore, once you enroll full-time you have 5 years of academic eligibility in which to complete 4 years of athletic eligibility.

What is needed to determine academic eligibility?

In order to compete in the NCAA student-athletes must graduate from high school and write a standardized test such as the SAT or ACT. For Division I and II students must then register with the NCAA Clearinghouse and be "cleared", both academically and athletically to compete in university athletics.

How does the NCAA determine overall academic eligibility?

NCCA minimum academic standards are determined based on the following sliding scale. Note that the high school average corresponding to a specific GPA and SAT will vary slightly from province to province.

What high school average is required to be academically eligible for NCAA?

A Canadian student-athlete will be considered to have satisfied the high school average requirements based on the following criteria for each province.

• Alberta - the student has obtained an Alberta High School Diploma with an average of at least 50% (equivalent to U.S. 2.000) or higher in all core-course areas.

• British Columbia - the student has obtained one of the following with an average of at least 50% (equivalent to U.S. 2.000) or higher in all core-course areas.

• Manitoba - the student presents a transcript indicating graduation from grade 12 with an average of at least 56% (equivalent to U.S. 2.000) or higher in all core-course areas.

• Saskatchewan - the student has received a Record of High School Standing-Grade 12 issued by the Saskatchewan Department of Education with an average of at least 60% (equivalent to U.S. 2.000) or higher in all core-course areas.

Do upgraded courses count in determining NCAA academic eligibility?

Yes. Upgraded courses taken by Canadian students in their home school systems can be used to determine NCAA eligibility.

SAT I: Reasoning Test

What is the SAT?

The SAT is a three-hour test that measures mathematical, critical reading and writing skills. Many colleges and universities use the SAT as one indicator of a student's readiness to perform college-level work. SAT scores are compared with the scores of other applicants and the accepted scores at an institution. For more on-line sample questions and preparation materials, visit www.collegboard.com.

Note: It is important to note that once you enroll "full-time" in college or university you can no longer write the SAT.

What subjects does the SAT cover?

There are three sections on the current version of the SAT.

• Writing Section: Multiple choice questions and a written essay
• Critical Reading: Both short and long reading passages
• Math: Expanded to include 3rd year high school material

How is the SAT scored?

The SAT is score out of a total of 2400. Each section of the SAT (math, critical reading and writing) is scored on a scale of 200-800. If the SAT is written more than once, the highest math score, the highest verbal score and the highest writing score will be combined to create the highest overall score.

What is the average score on the SAT?

For students entering college in 2003, the average reading score is 508 and the average math score is 518. Because the writing section is new there are no reliable average numbers for comparison.

Will the NCAA be using the writing section to determine NCAA eligibility?

No. For the time being the NCAA will continue to use only the math and critical reading sections in determining NCAA eligibility – sections that correspond to the math and verbal sections of the previous version of the SAT. However, it is important to note that although the NCAA may not be using the writing section in determining eligibility member universities are free to use it in assessing student-athlete applicants.

Where is the SAT offered?

The SAT is offered at a number of locations throughout North America and in all major cities. Visit www.collegeboard.com to determine the nearest location.

How do I register for the SAT?

Go to www.collegeboard.com and follow the directions provided under the SAT tab

How many times can I write the SAT?

There is no limit to the number of times that a student can write the SAT, however only 6 scores will appear on the SAT score report.

How many times should I write the SAT?

You should write the SAT at least 2 times. Since the SAT is a very unique test, prior experience writing and studying for the test will help you perform better on subsequent attempts. Also, because you can combine your highest math, critical reading and writing sections from all tests the more tests that you write the more likely it is that you will perform better in one of these areas.

How do I study for the SAT?

The most effective way to prepare for the SAT is to purchase an SAT study guide available at most book stores. These study aids are extremely useful for learning how to write the test and in becoming familiar with the exam format and question types. There are also several agencies that have programs built specific for learning how to write this difficult exam.

Can I write the SAT while attending university or college?

Yes, as long as you are not classified as a "full-time" student as per that institutions definition of "full time". You must be classified as a "part-time" student.

SAT II: Subject Tests (SAT II)

What is the SAT II?

The SAT II's are one-hour, mostly multiple-choice, individual tests that measure how much students know about a particular academic subject and how well they can apply that knowledge. Many colleges require or recommend one or more of the subject tests for admission and student-athletes will be advised as to whether they have to write them or not.

Which SAT II's should I take?

Unless the university specifies which SAT II's you must take, choose the tests based on your subject strengths and the amount of time since you studied that particular topic.

How are SAT II's scored?

SAT II scores are reported on a scale from 200 to 800.

When should you take the SAT II's?

Most students take the SAT II's toward the end of grade 11 or at the beginning of grade 12. Take tests such as world history, biology, chemistry, or physics as soon as possible after completing the course in the subject, while the material is still fresh in your mind.

How do I register for the SAT II's?

• Online: Go to www.collegeboard.com and follow the directions provided under the SAT tab • Mail: To register by mail, you need a *Registration Bulletin* which is available at your school counselor's office. The Registration Form and return envelope are included in the *Registration Bulletin*. Your completed registration form must be returned in the envelope provided with proper payment.

Registration Bulletin contains test dates, registration deadlines, fees, instructions, test center codes, and other registration-related information.

How do I study for the SAT II's?

Because the SAT II's focus on specific subject areas The most effective way to prepare for specific SAT II subject tests is to study for similar high school courses and purchase SAT II study guides available at some book stores.

What's the difference between the SAT and Subject Tests?

The SAT tests general aptitude in math and English where as the SAT II's test knowledge in specific subject areas. The SAT is required to compete in the NCAA while the SAT II's are required at the discretion of individual universities.

ACT

What is the ACT?

The ACT is (a) a set of four multiple-choice tests which cover English, mathematics, reading, and science, and (b) an optional writing section

What subjects does the ACT cover?

The ACT covers the following subjects:

- English, 75 questions, 45 minutes
- Math, 60 questions, 60 minutes
- Reading, 40 questions, 35 minutes
- Science, 40 questions, 35 minutes
- Optional Writing Test, 1 question, 30 Minutes

How do I register for the ACT?

To register for the ACT got to www.act.org. All Canadian students will have to register by mail so download, complete and return the "registration packet."

How do I study for the ACT?

The best preparation for the ACT is preparation for high school curriculum—courses in English, math, science, and social studies. For practice questions and tests go to www.act.org or purchase a study guides for the ACT from a book store.

How is the ACT scored?

Both the combined score (overall score) and each test score (English, math, reading, science) range from 1 (low) to 36 (high). The combined score is the average of your four test scores, rounded to the nearest whole number.

Which scores are reported if I test more than once?

There is a separate record for each test and only test scores that are requested are released to universities. Unlike the SAT, you may not select test scores from different test dates to construct a new record; you must designate an entire test date record as it stands. ACT does not create new records by averaging scores from different test dates.

What is the difference between the ACT and SAT?

The ACT is an achievement test, measuring what a student has learned in school. The SAT is more of an aptitude test, testing reasoning and verbal abilities. The ACT has up to 5 components: English, Mathematics, Reading, Science, and an optional Writing Test. The SAT has only 3 components: verbal, math, and a writing test. Math makes up 50% of SAT's test score and only 25% of ACT's test score.

Who should take the SAT and who should take the ACT?

Students who have recently graduated or are near graduation may perform better on the ACT as it focuses on specific subject areas studied in high school. Students who have been out of high school for a year or more may perform better on the SAT as it tests for general reasoning and aptitude.

ATHLETIC ELIGIBILITY

Amateurism, What is amateurism?

In order to compete in the NCAA student-athletes must be classified as "amateurs" by the NCAA. To remain an "amateur" you cannot compete or sign a contract with a professional team, accept money or gifts for athletic ability retain the services of an agent, or receive money for educational expenses based on athletic ability.

How many years of athletic eligibility do I have to compete in NCAA athletics?

You have four (4) years of athletic eligibility in the NCAA.

Major Junior (WHL, OHL, QMJHL)

Can I play games in major junior and still be eligible to compete in the NCAA?

The NCAA considers major junior hockey to be professional hockey. Therefore student-athletes who compete in Major Junior jeopardize some or all of their NCAA athletic eligibility because they fail to remain "amateurs" as per NCAA regulations. Student-athletes will lose all athletic eligibility to compete in NCAA Division I hockey if they: • compete in any major junior game after their expected date of high school graduation, or • sign a contract ("WHL Player Agreement") with a major junior team Student athletes will lose some athletic eligibility to compete in NCAA Division I hockey if they:
 • compete in any major junior game before their expected date of high school graduation, without signing a contract, or attend a major junior training camp for more than 48 hours while having their expenses covered by the major junior team The only scenario in what a player can compete in major junior and still retain NCAA athletic eligibility is if he plays an exhibition game before graduating from high school without ever having signed a player agreement. Any other competition in major junior will lead to the loss of all NCAA athletic eligibility.

Can I tryout for teams in major junior and still be eligible to compete in the NCAA?

Before enrollment in a NCAA University an athlete can: Tryout for any length of time with a professional or major junior hockey team at your own expense. Receive one expense paid tryout with a professional or major junior team as long as it does not exceed 48 hours. (Note: You can only receive 1 expenses paid tryout from each team.)

RESERVED

Note that during a tryout, an individual loses NCAA athletic eligibility if he takes part in any outside competition as a representative of that major junior team (games, scrimmages, 3-on-3 tournaments, etc.).

Does the major junior rule apply to Division II and III?

Although the rule varies slightly between divisions, competition at the major junior level may jeopardize eligibility to compete in all NCAA divisions. For more specific information concerning how the rule is applied to Division II and III visit www.ncaa.org.

21-Year Old Rule
What happens if I turn 21 years old during the junior hockey season?

If you play a junior hockey game after your 21st birthday you will lose 1 year of NCAA athletic eligibility leaving you with 3 years remaining.

Does this rule apply to Division II and III?

No. This rule applies only to Division I.

How can I turn 21 years old, continue playing junior hockey and still retain NCAA eligibility?

Using the NCAA "transfer rules" you can continue playing junior hockey after your 21st birthday and retain 4 years of athletic eligibility if, prior to competing after your 21st birthday, you enroll full-time at a college institution that does not sponsor a hockey program. Although you will lose some of your 5-year academic eligibility you will not lose any of your 4-year athletic eligibility.

When should I enroll full-time if I want to continue playing junior hockey after my 21st birthday?

In order to avoid the hassle of registration when the hockey season is busy, you should enroll full-time in September. Also, in order to avoid difficulties with the NCAA Clearinghouse, you should register with the Clearinghouse before enrolling full-time. It is important to note that once you enroll "full-time" in college or university you can no longer write the SAT.

Does the rule apply to Division II and III?

No. The 21-year old rule applies only to student-athletes wishing to compete in Division I. It does not apply to those student-athletes wishing to compete in Division II and III.

RECRUITING

Promoting
What do university coaches look for when they recruit student-athletes?

In making decisions on prospective players, Universities will consider the entire profile of the student athlete. That profile includes academic qualities such as high school marks, SAT or ACT scores, as well as athletic and personal qualities such as skill, attitude, and work ethic. What qualities are most important depends on the needs of the individual university and hockey program.

How do I best promote myself to NCAA hockey programs?

The most effective way to promote you is to develop a well-rounded student-athlete profile. Start by taking and performing well in proper high school classes, studying for and achieving a high score on the SAT or ACT and working hard on developing as an athlete.

Can I contact NCAA hockey programs and coaches?

Yes. You can contact university and coaches at any point and there are no restrictions on the time or content of the contact.

Should I send a hockey resume to NCAA hockey programs to help promote myself?

Although sending a resume will not hurt your chances of getting a scholarship, its effectiveness is very limited. University hockey coaches are professional scouts and most programs employ a full-time recruiter. These recruiters spend many hours in arenas watching and interviewing student-athletes and are less inclined to read a student-athlete resume.

However, schools that do not have a lot of resources devoted to actively recruiting prospects, such as Division III and smaller Division I universities, are more open to student-athlete resumes. However, if you decide to send a student-athlete resume make sure that it is no longer than 1 page and includes only relevant information such as SAT, high school average and hockey statistics.

B. Recruiting Guidelines

When can universities start contacting and recruiting?

University hockey coaches can contact you or your parent's once during the month of July after grade 10 and once in grade 11. After July 1 of the summer between grade 11 and grade 12 college coaches may contact you once a week throughout the year.

What is an "official visit" or "fly-down"?

An "official visit" or "fly-down" is a visit to a university campus paid for by the university or hockey program. Fly-downs are used by athletics programs to introduce you to the university and members of the team, give you a flavor for the campus and induce you to attend their university.

How many official visits can I make?

You can receive a maximum of 5 official visits but may only visit each campus once.

What are the rules concerning official visits?

In order to make an official visit you must have started classes in grade 12. Also, before a university can bring you to campus on a visit you must provide high school transcripts and a completed SAT or ACT score. Each official visit may last no longer than 48 hours and can cover food, entertainment, lodging and transportation.

Canadian Interuniversity Sport (CIS)

What is the CIS?

The CIS is the governing body for Canadian university athletics.

How many universities offer hockey programs?

There are 3 regional associations in CIS hockey comprised of a total of 30 university hockey programs:

1. Canada West
- University of Lethbridge
- University of Saskatchewan
- University of Regina
- University of B.C.
- University of Calgary
- University of Alberta
- University of Manitoba

2. Atlantic Region
- University of New Brunswick
- St. Francis Xavier
- Saint Mary's University
- Dalhousie University
- Acadia University
- University of P.E.I.
- Université de Moncton

3. Ontario University Association
- Royal Military College
- University of Western Ontario
- University of Waterloo
- University of Toronto
- Ryerson University

- Queen's University
- University of Ottawa
- Université du Québec à Trois-rivières
- Laurier
- McGill University
- Concordia University
- University of Guelph
- York
- Brock University
- University of Windsor

Scholarships/Financial Assistance

Can CIS universities offer financial awards or scholarships for athletic competition?

Yes. CIS universities can offer financial assistance/scholarships for university athletic participation within certain restrictions and guidelines as set out by the CIS.

What is the definition of financial awards?

The CIS refers to its scholarships and financial assistance as "Athletic Financial Awards" (AFA). An AFA is any award that is conditional on the student participating as a member of an athletic team. These awards include but are not limited to scholarships, bursaries, prizes, leadership awards, merit awards, housing, and all other related non-employment financial benefit received by an athlete from their institution.

Who is eligible for an AFA?

Both students entering their first year of university and students who have all ready competed for the university are eligible for financial assistance.

What are the eligibility requirements for an AFA?

Students who are considered "entering students" must achieve a minimum 80% grade average in the previous academic year of study in order to be eligible for university financial assistance. An "entering student" is any student who has not yet completed two (2) semesters of study at the CIS institution they are currently attending. This definition includes students entering from high school, students who are currently in their first year of university, as well as students who transfer from another post-secondary institution.

Students who are considered "non-entering students" must achieve a 65% G.P.A. within the previous academic year of study. A "non-entering student" is any student who has successfully completed two (2) semester of study at the institution they are currently attending. This would include second, third, fourth and fifth year university students.

Is there a maximum number of AFA's that an individual student-athlete can receive?

Although there are no restrictions on the number of AFA's that a student-athlete may receive in one academic year, the aggregate amount of the AFA's received by any one student can total no more than the cost of tuition and compulsory fees.

Is there a maximum amount of money that can be given out by a university in the form of AFA's?

Yes. Using a complicated formula, each CIS hockey team is allowed 14 AFA units. One (1) AFA unit accounts for 100% of one athlete's tuition and compulsory fees. For example, if your tuition and compulsory fees total $5,000, and the university awards you an AFA totaling $5,000, then they have used one (1) AFA unit on you. If you receive $2,500 then only 0.5 AFA units have been used on you.

Therefore, 14 AFA's units allows for 14 players to receive 100% of their tuition and compulsory fees. Conversely, 7 players could receive 100% of their tuition and compulsory fees while 14 players receive 50% of their tuition and compulsory fees. Each individual CIS hockey team decides how it will divide its 14 AFA's among its student-athletes. Also, it must be noted that schools are not required to give away all 14 AFA's each year. Some universities may award the full 14 AFA's while others may award none – the decision rests with each individual university.

ACADEMIC ELIGIBILITY
A. High School Requirements
What high school average is required to be academically eligible for CIS?

A prospective student-athlete must obtain a minimum 60% average on those courses used to determine university admission. It must be noted that this only makes the student eligible to compete in CIS athletics and does not guarantee entrance into a specific university or program.

What happens if I don't have a 60% average but get accepted into a CIS institution?

In those instances where you have not achieved the 60% requirement, but nonetheless have been accepted into a CIS university, you must complete 9 credit hours or equivalent in a single semester prior to gaining eligibility.

B. Continued CIS Eligibility

What is required in order to continue to be eligible to compete in the CIS?

In order to be eligible to continue competing in CIS athletics you must have successfully completed 3 full courses in the previous semester and be enrolled in 3 full courses during the current semester.

ATHLETIC ELIGIBILITY

Athletic Eligibility

How many years of athletic eligibility do I have to compete in CIS athletics?

Every student-athlete has five (5) years to compete in CIS athletics.

What is considered a "year of competition" in the CIS?

If your name appears on a playing roster for one or more regular season games in one season then you are considered to have "participated" or "competed" for 1 season.

Does ACAC and NCAA competition count towards my five (5) years of CIS athletic eligibility?

Yes. For each year of competition in either the ACAC or NCAA you are charged with a year of eligibility according to that jurisdiction's rules. Within the ACAC or NCAA an athlete shall be charged with a year of CIS eligibility in accordance with the ACAC or NCAA definition of "competition", "participation" and "eligibility".

Also, athletes who have used all of their ACAC or NCAA athletic eligibility are ineligible to compete in the CIS.

HOCKEY DEVELOPMENT CAMPS

Amateurism

Do I lose CIS athletic eligibility if I compete for a professional team, play in a professional league or get paid to play hockey?

For each year that you played professional hockey you will lose one of your five years of CIS eligibility.

Do exhibition games count as professional competition?

No. Hockey players are not considered to have competed professional regardless of the number of exhibition games played.

How soon after competing professional can I take part in CIS athletics?

One year must pass between your last professional competition and your first game in the CIS.

Do I lose CIS athletic eligibility if I tryout for a professional team?

No. As long as you do not compete in a game in a professional league you will not lose any eligibility for participation in a tryout.

C. Major Junior (WHL, OHL, QMJHL)

Can I play games in major junior and still be eligible to compete in the CIS?

Yes. Unlike the NCAA, the CIS does not consider major junior hockey leagues to be professional hockey leagues and therefore competition in these leagues will not jeopardize CIS athletic eligibility.

Can I tryout for teams in major junior and still be eligible to compete in the CIS?

Yes. Unlike the NCAA, participation in major junior hockey tryouts will not jeopardize any CIS eligibility.

Transferring to the CIS

Does ACAC and NCAA competition count towards my five (5) years of CIS athletic eligibility?

Yes. For each year of competition in either the ACAC or NCAA you are charged with a year of eligibility according to that jurisdiction's rules. Within the ACAC or NCAA an athlete shall be charged with a year of CIS eligibility in accordance with the ACAC or NCAA definition of "competition", "participation" and "eligibility".

If I transfer from the ACAC, how soon after I transfer can I play?
If you transfer from the ACAC to the CIS you may play immediately if:
1. you have not participated in any ACAC contest that semester;
2. you have achieved a 60% average in the ACAC courses used to determine CIS eligibility; and
3. you have not used all of your ACAC eligibility.

If I transfer from the NCAA, how soon after I transfer can I play?
If you transfer from the NCAA and
1. you have achieved a 60% average in the NCAA courses, or subsequent courses, used to determine CIS eligibility; and;
2. you have not used all of your NCAA eligibility then one year must pass from your last NCAA hockey game before you will be eligible to compete in the CIS.

Can I transfer and compete in the CIS if I have used all my eligibility in the ACAC or NCAA?
In general, if you have used all of your athletic eligibility in the ACAC or NCAA then you cannot compete in the CIS. However, NCAA athletes who participated for three years or less in the NCAA, but are no longer eligible in the NCAA because of the NCAA time-clock/age limit or terms of attendance regulations, may compete in the CIS using their remaining CIS eligibility.

RECRUITING

Recruiting Guidelines
Do CIS universities provide for recruiting trips?
Yes. Universities can bring prospective student athletes to campus for recruiting trips.

Can a CIS university cover prospect travel expenses for recruiting trips?
University funding of recruiting trips for prospective athletes is acceptable providing these trips are consistent with general university policy.

How many official visits can I make?
Although there is no limit on the number of universities you can visit on financed recruiting trips, each university can provide for only one financed recruiting trip per prospective athlete.

Can CIS universities pay for my parents to visit the campus?

No. CIS universities are prohibited from paying, providing, or arranging for the payment of transportation costs incurred by relatives or friends of a prospective athlete.

Can I receive university apparel or other products while on a recruiting trip?

Yes you can receive university products or services provided the products or services do not exceed $50.00 over and above what is provided the general prospective student population.

Alberta Colleges Athletics Conference (ACAC) & Canadian Colleges Athletics Association (CCAA)

What is the CCAA?

The CCAA is the governing body for Canadian collegiate sports.

What is the ACAC?

The ACAC is the governing body for collegiate hockey in Alberta. The ACAC is permitted to make regulations provided they are consistent with or more restrictive than those made by the CCAA.

How many ACAC hockey programs are there?

There are seven (7) ACAC hockey programs:
• Augustana University College, U of A (AUC)
• Briercrest College (BC)
• Concordia University College of Alberta (CUCA)
• MacEwan College (MacEwan)
• Mount Royal College (MRC)
• Northern Alberta Institute of Technology (NAIT)
• SAIT Polytechnic (SAIT)

Financial Assistance

Can ACAC institutions offer financial awards or scholarships to its student-athletes?

Yes. ACAC institutions can offer financial assistance to its athletes.

What is the definition of financial assistance?

Financial assistance includes scholarships, bursaries, grants and financial awards.

Who is eligible for an athletic financial assistance?

Any student who competes in athletics and meets the requirements for financial assistance can receive financial assistance. Each institution sets its own eligibility requirements for athletic assistance.

Is there a maximum amount of assistance that individual student-athletes can receive?

Yes. Financial assistance or awards cannot exceed the total cost of the student-athlete's enrollment fees.

What is the definition of "enrollment fees"?

Enrollment fees shall include tuition, recreation fees, Student Association fees, etc.

ACADEMIC ELIGIBILITY

High School Requirements

What are the academic requirements in order to be eligible to compete in the ACAC?

There are no minimum high school requirements set out by the CCAA or the ACAC to determine initial athletic eligibility. Each individual institution sets the entrance requirements of its students and as far as the ACAC is concerned if a student is admitted to the institution then he/she is eligible to compete in the ACAC. Therefore, initial academic requirements will be dependant on the program of study and institution to which you are applying.

B. Continued ACAC Eligibility

What are the academic requirements to be eligible to continue competing in the ACAC?

Once attending an ACAC institution and competing in athletics, a student-athlete must maintain "full-time" status and achieve a passing G.P.A. each semester in order to be eligible to compete in the following semester.

What is a full-time student?

A student shall be considered full-time if he/she is officially registered in a minimum of 60% of a full course load in an accredited program of study.

Who determines what is "full-time" and what is a "passing G.P.A."?

Each individual institution shall determine what constitutes a full-time student and what constitutes a passing G.P.A.

ATHLETIC ELIGIBILITY

How many years of athletic eligibility do I have to compete in ACAC athletics?

You have four (4) years to compete in the ACAC.

What is considered "a year of competition"?

You will be considered to have used one year of eligibility if you have participated in one scheduled ACAC contest. This does not include preseason contests.

Can I attend two ACAC institutions and still take part in the athletics programs?

Yes. Students registered in more than one institution simultaneously shall be free to choose the institution for their athletic participation. You must declare an institution as your "home campus" for athletic purposes prior to the first scheduled conference competition.

Amateurism

Do I lose ACAC athletic eligibility if I compete for a professional team, play in a professional league or get paid to play hockey?

No. Unlike the NCAA and CIS, participation as a professional hockey player does not affect the number of years of ACAC athletic eligibility.

Do I lose ACAC athletic eligibility if I tryout for a professional team?

No. Hockey players are allowed to tryout for professional hockey teams without jeopardizing their ACAC eligibility.

C. Major Junior (WHL, OHL, QMJHL)

Can I play games in major junior and still be eligible to compete in the ACAC?

Yes. Unlike the NCAA, the ACAC does not consider major junior hockey leagues to be professional hockey leagues. Therefore, competition in these leagues will not jeopardize any ACAC eligibility.

Can I tryout for teams in major junior and still be eligible to compete in the ACAC?

Yes. Unlike the NCAA, participation in major junior hockey tryouts will not jeopardize any ACAC eligibility.

D. Transferring to the ACAC

Does NCAA and CIS participation count towards the four (4) years of my ACAC eligibility?

Yes. Participation in the NCAA or CIS will be considered equivalent to and deducted from your four years of ACAC eligibility. The NCAA and CIS definitions of "competition", "participation" and "eligibility" will be respected in determining loss of ACAC eligibility. As an example, if you entered the NCAA and played 10 games in your first season then, according to NCAA definitions, you would have "competed" and as such used one (1) year of NCAA "eligibility". Therefore, if you transfer to the ACAC you would have only three (3) years of ACAC eligibility remaining.

If I transfer from the NCAA or CIS, how soon after I transfer can I play?

If you transfer between seasons of your sport (i.e. during the summer) you will be eligible to compete immediately if you satisfy one of the following: you met the academic standard for athletic participation during the last semester of full-time attendance at the NCAA or CIS institution from which you are transferring; or

2. You have attended your new ACAC institution for a full term (minimum 12 weeks) during which your sport has been playing, but you only practiced and competed in exhibition games. If you transfer from an NCAA or CIS institution for which you competed in hockey during the same sport year, you will be deemed ineligible to compete in ACAC hockey for the remainder of that sport year. For example, if you played a game in the CIS in October of 2004 and transferred to an ACAC institution in January, you would not be eligible to play at the ACAC institution until September of 2005 – the start of a new sport year.

Can I transfer from one ACAC institution to another ACAC institution and still play?

If you transfer between seasons of your sport (i.e. during the summer) you will be eligible to compete immediately if you satisfy one of the following:

a. You met the academic standard for athletic participation during the last semester of full-time attendance at the NCAA or CIS institution from which you are transferring; or

b. You have attended your new ACAC institution for a full term (minimum 12 weeks) during which your sport has been playing, but you only practiced and competed in exhibition games.

If you transfer from an ACAC institution for which you competed in hockey during the same sport year, you will be deemed ineligible to compete in ACAC hockey for the remainder of that sport year. For example, if you played a game in the ACAC in October of 2004 and transferred to another ACAC institution in January, you would not be eligible to play at the new ACAC institution until September of 2005 – the start of a new sport year.

RECRUITING

A. Recruiting Guidelines
Do ACAC institutions provide for recruiting trips?

Students are free to visit the campus of an ACAC institution at any time.

How many official visits can I make?

There are no restrictions on the number of times you can visit an ACAC campus.

Can an ACAC/CCAA institution cover prospect expenses for recruiting trips?

No. No institution shall finance transportation costs incurred by a prospective student-athlete. Moreover, no institution shall finance, arrange or permit entertainment of any prospective student-athletes.

Can ACAC/CCAA universities pay for my parents to visit the campus?

No. No institution shall finance transportation costs incurred by his/her family or friends.

Can I receive apparel or other products while on a recruiting trip?

No. No institution shall finance, arrange or permit the giving of gifts to prospective student-athletes.

Preparing For Tomorrow Today

The Key to being recruited as a college athlete is getting an early start in the process and realizing that the process takes several years of preparation in order to be successful.

Grade 10: Age 15 to 16

- Focus on educational planning. Remember to concentrate on achieving good grades, especially in your core academic courses, since grade 10 academic courses may be used to calculate grade-point average for admissions to US post secondary schools.
- Start searching entrance requirements for both Canadian and American Colleges & Universities. **It is very important to research your options!**
- Research information about the SAT Admissions Test, including how Canadian students register to write at a Canadian testing location.
- Research the specific recruiting regulations established by the NCAA, the NAIA, the CIS, and the CCAA. Register with the NCAA at **WWW.COLLEGEBOARD.COM**

Begin preparing your resume. Consider volunteer and extracurricular activities that would help in attaining financial awards. Also begin to search financial scholarship/awards criteria.

Grade 11: Age 16 to 17
Monitor and tailor your educational plan. Remember to concentrate on achieving high academic grades, since grade 11 academic courses are used to calculate grade-point average for admissions to US post secondary schools.

- Write the SAT exam. **The higher the grade-point average and SAT score, the more options will be available.**
- Update your resume and begin to market yourself to US & Canadian College & Universities.

Continue your research on scholarship/awards.

- **Grade 12: Age 17 to 18**

- Rewrite the SAT exam if necessary. Many students write the exam more than once in order to achieve the combined score necessary for admissions.
- Obtain all necessary registration forms and ensure that all documents are completed and submitted prior to deadline dates.

Opening the Doors of Opportunity

Student athletes do not want to make the mistake of waiting for recruiters to come to them. Student athletes also do not want to wait until their grade 12 year to begin the process of creating options.

The world of marketing and advertising has shown us that product awareness and recognition are the most important factors for product success. Likewise, those athletes who get mentioned the most in the media or in a game reports are the ones that coaches hear about the most.

They can't recruit you if they don't know you exist. If you follow the steps below, your chances of being recruited will be greatly enhanced.

Register with the NCAA clearinghouse: All students' athletes that want to compete in NCAA Division I or III levels in their freshman year must register to determine eligibility.

Write the SAT or ACT exam: Both are standardized exams that are used to determine how suitable a prospective student athlete is to a 1st year program of a post-secondary institution in the US.

1. **High School transcript**: Consult your high school counselor. An official copy of your final transcript needs to be sent directly from your high school to the NCAA clearinghouse for eligibility review in order to participate in the US collegiate competition. Canadian post-secondary require an official copy of your transcript in order to determine admission.

2. **Write a letter of introduction:** It should be brief and addressed to the coach. It should express the student's interest in both the academic and athletic program at the post-secondary institution and refer to an enclosed resume.

3. **Develop a resume:** It should be a complete inventory of academic, athletic, social, extra-curricular and community accomplishments and list references.

4. **Letters of recommendation:** Consult your coach.

5. **Make a video:** This may be the only way a coach can separate one prospect from another. Start filming at the beginning of the season and include a 15 minute portion from a game plus highlights from different games. Begin with an on-camera introduction of you, by you, and just try to be sincere **(Don't try to be funny or outrageous.)**

Follow up letters: These are used to make sure that the coach has received your first letter and also to put you back on top of the pile to remind the coach that you are still interested. Include a copy of your first letter, your resume, and any newspaper clippings, updated stats, etc.

Even with all the information provided, it is best to go into your guidance counselor and meet with them to discuss what steps to take and let them know your intentions. It may seem very early, sand it is, but it must be done, and the more help you have from your guidance counselor the easier the process will go. DO NOT BE THE ATHLETE THAT HAS ALL THE ATHLETIC ABILITY, BUT DOES NOT QUALIFY ACADEMICALLY FOR A SCHOLARSHIP.

NCAA Eligibility Center address: P.O. Box 7136, Indianapolis, IN 4620

CHAPTER 8
CAN ATHLETES MAKE IT PLAYING IN A SMALLER ORGANIZATION?

This is a widely discussed subject and always seems to get blown out of proportion. This topic will enter your household at some point, if you child happens to be an exceptional athlete. Unfortunately this topic always comes up to early, and becomes a focal point for the parent's and then the child. In all cases the idea that for your player to succeed; they must move to a bigger organization in order to get the exposure from the scouts, and to have the best coaching available. This statement is simply not true. The real issue is how this babble festers through every small minor hockey organization, at every age. It is openly discussed in front of the kids and it becomes the biggest distraction to the children playing this simple game. I consider myself a professional at this subject, because I personally have been through this ordeal as a player.

When I was in Bantam my 1ˢᵗ year, I was playing in a small single AA organization, my parents continued to be my biggest supporters, but what they didn't realize is that during this time in my life they were also a very big distraction. I was lead to believe by my parents, that in order for me to have any success, I needed to move to a bigger center. Why did I believe this nonsense? Because they were my parents, and they always were looking out for my best interest, or so I thought.

I as all players had the dream of playing hockey at the highest level possible. After having a good game, instead of enjoying the win and the excitement of the game, My dad would start talking about how that even though my game was good, he quickly would point out that a am not doing it at the highest level meaning a AAA organization like Penticton. The nearest town that had AAA hockey, and my dad one way or the other was going to make sure that I got that opportunity. I started to believe that In order to succeed, I must move and play minor hockey in Penticton. This Idea consumed my every thought. It started to affect my attitude towards the organization I was playing in.

Hockey is the greatest sport in the world, but it can sure take your emotions onto a major rollercoaster ride. Even though my dad new deep down that it would be almost impossible for me to play in Penticton because of very strict player boundaries, he spoke about it and so did several other parents It became this monster and a negative in my life. I started feeling that next year would be a waste if I didn't move on to Penticton. This went on for the next year, what should have been my best year 2ⁿᵈ year of bantam AA where I was named the captain. Our team won the league, the playoffs, and we went right to the Provincial Final game. But somehow it just wasn't good enough; I could still hear my dad talking about my success is still just at the AA level. Not knowing any better, I continued to doubt my skills as an athlete.

The next year my parents along with one other family, decided to challenge the rules of hockey. The rule was simply this; you must play in the association in your hometown if the association had declared that they were going to have a rep team no matter the level, A, AA, or AAA.

The only way I was going to be able to play in another community was to move to that town. At that time we didn't need to be going to school in Penticton, but you must have a physical address to register for the upcoming hockey season. So what my family did with one other family in Summerland is rented a motel suite in Penticton, for the winter.

Our Address was the Shore line Motel in Penticton. We rented this hotel in August so we had a physical address, then we could apply to Penticton minor hockey and tryout for the AAA team. A bit of a risk as if I didn't make the team, I'm not sure where I would be playing.

Going through the tryout process I soon showed the coaches that I could play at this level and be a major contributor. I was named an assistant captain and felt very comfortable in my new surroundings; our team was very competitive and was winning most of its games. At Christmas we were getting ready to go to a major tournament in Quebec, something that our team was looking forward to. About 2 weeks before our departure, my friend and I from Summerland were dealt the most disturbing blow. We were cut from the team for not following the residency rules, as we were not actually living in Penticton, we only were renting a hotel their by breaking the rules in place by the governing body of minor hockey The way we got caught, well that is another whole chapter that I will not get into. Let's just say that there were some Penticton parents that were upset that we were on their hockey team, which displaced some of the local players.

We were both forced to go back to Summerland mid season and we were very fortunate that the team in Summerland welcomed us back with no problems, except that in order for us to get on this team, they needed to cut a couple of players. As a youngster I didn't think much about the situation, but now I can only imagine the heartbreak that these players must of felt as they were both friends of mine. Even today I still think about that year, and how it impacted so many parents and players in so many ways, because my parents and I thought that I was going nowhere if I didn't get to the next level of play.

Here is my point, after returning to Summerland I realized that the hockey was not much different at all. We went on that year to place 3rd in the province and ended up having one of the best second half seasons in my life. Tim and I both got to go on to play junior hockey.

Tim played Junior A and then went on to a Division 3 College where he won a National Championship his senior year as the captain. He is currently a head coach at the Division 3 level and has won a National Title there as a coach. I played Junior B and soon realized that I didn't have the dedication or desire to move up the ladder of hockey, something I still regret to this day.

But the one thing that I learned through that whole or deal is that you do not need to move to make it to the highest level of hockey, you just need the attitude and the desire to do so. Scouts are at all games, at all levels, and if you are good enough, you will be seen and get your chance.

I did some research within the Western Hockey League and most scouts I talked to, love to find that diamond in the rough, Scouts take pride in locating players in remote areas. Shea Webber came from a small town that had around 2000 people. A small Single A association, so it does happen all the time. Parents always remember it is the athlete himself that will make it not the environment that he plays under at the minor hockey level. There will come a time that your child will need to make a decision to move to play Junior hockey, and that decision will be difficult enough on its own.

Once you get to the Junior level, hockey becomes a business and most times you may be forced to move away from home to pursue your dream. The main things the parents can do are to stay patient, be supportive and knowledgeable in the Minor Hockey Association you are involved with. Let your child grow as a person, keep hockey fun and they will be successful no matter how far they go in their chosen sport.

HOCKEY DEVELOPMENT CAMPS

CHAPTER 9
HELPING YOUR CHILD MAKE EDUCATED HOCKEY DECISIONS

Hockey, as all sports, requires a lot of understanding about exactly how the system works. As parents, we all want to make good educated decisions. But a lot of times we get blinded by the first person that shows any interest in our child as an athlete. Rule number one. Never overreact to any interest in your son or daughter, take all the information in and go back home and do your homework and find out all the pertinent information.

Look up the team on the internet, if it is a junior team; find out how many players are leaving the team this year because of ageing out or Scholarship opportunities. Through this research you will be able to find out several things: Are there yearly NCAA scholarships given to the team, and which schools tend to take players from this team? Are players playing on the team for more that 1 year? This will tell you something about the coach and his relationship with his players. Don't forget, just because a Scout or a team representative has shown some interest in your child, does not mean that they are going to be playing there. All scouts are interested in Potential players for their respective organizations. Scouts and managers especially good ones are very good salesmen, they make it sound like your son is the next Wayne Gretsky. The one main thing that all hockey players need to develop their skills is ice time. Remember this when you are looking at different levels of junior hockey for your son. You could be a player that is in and out of the lineup at the Canadian Hockey league level or even the Junior A level, some thought must be put into the possibility of playing a year at the Junior B level or lower, where you can be a contributing player plus getting lots of valuable ice time and confidence.

Working as the international Development Tournament Coordinator in Penticton, we always had professional guest speakers. During one of the lectures, Chuck Kobesew who currently plays for the Boston Bruins was asked. "What do you think helped you the most in your journey to the NHL?" Chuck said, without a doubt, was his decision to not rush his junior career. He played a year and a half of Junior B hockey in his hometown Osoyoos. When he was recruited by the Penticton Panther's of the British Columbia Hockey League. He was offered a chance to play there as a very young player, Chuck with his family decided that he would get more ice time at the Junior B level and stay at home , which he did. Chuck moved on half way through the next season to play in Penticton he did so only when he felt he could be a contributor at that level. He finished the year in Penticton playing 30 games and getting 27 points. Chuck continued to reinforce to the kids, he wasn't going to make the jump to the next level of play unless he felt he could contribute to his new team which he certainly did.

The following year Chuck scored over 106 points in 58 games for the Penticton Panthers. Chuck played a year and a half at both the Junior B and A levels Then Chuck received a Scholarship at Boston College, he also came back to play a year in Kelowna with the Kelowna Rockets of the WHL.

This speech from Chuck was very uplifting to all 220 players in our tournament. This was one of the most powerful speeches these young players have ever heard. The kids came out of the auditorium thinking in a very positive direction. Many of these young players are pushed by their parents to play at such a high level, even though it may not be in the best interest of the player.

All athletes develop at different times and in much different ways, and you must consider the big picture. What is best for the individual player? Speak with the coaches from your organization, be approachable and get some straight answers regarding the best place for your athlete to play.

After speaking with hundreds of parents and players from around the world regarding this matter, one thing is very clear, the parents have a different view than the actual players. I asked the parent's one question. "What do you consider a successful year for your athlete"? The parents had two answers. The non competitive parent says as long as he has fun and stays healthy, that is all that matters. The Competitive parent always says playing at the highest level possible, trying to get the most exposure. The parents rationalize that if their son plays at a higher level, even if he is not actually ready for it, he will be forced to get better. These are all concepts that may not necessarily be true.

When asking the players the same question, their answers were very consistent. They do want to play at the highest level possible, but the other side of the coin they also said, **THEY WANT TO PLAY**, plus be a contributor on the team. If you look at the answers that were given, who is giving the best and most thought out answer.

I will let you make the judgment on it. Competitive players should always strive to play at the highest level, but keep in mind, that in order for them to get better, they must have fun and be able to play in a situation that they are going to get regular ice time in a safe and comfortable environment.

CHAPTER 10
WHO CAN GUIDE ME THROUGH MY CHILD'S HOCKEY DEVELOPMENT?

T his is a question that every parent needs to resolve. Some parents will listen to anyone that has something positive to say about their child, after all my kid is going to the NHL. The toughest realization parents need to make is what the actual skill level and desire of your child is. Parents see all the work and dedication that their kids show and immediately make the assumption that their son or daughter is destine to play in the NHL. I'm sure we have all had this discussion with our child about how great it would be to realize their dream and play in the NHL. Be careful in establishing that it is actually his dream and not yours, as there is a big difference. Parents don't realize that in a lot of ways we are blind when it come to our children. The one thing you can control as a parent is being the one to help your child go through the difficult process of realizing his own potential and helping him move forward without being a disruptive medaling parent.

We all like to say that we are not involved in our child's sporting life, but realize it or not, you are. You hold the key to success for your child, and that player since Wayne Gretsky. The level that your child will ultimately play will be decided by your son or daughter, and with the coaches and scouts that see your child play. What you can do is help him find the best teams to try out for. Do your research!

If your son is a forward, find out how many returning forwards there are, find out about the coaches philosophy, the program, and the costs to play. If it is a US or Canadian Midget program, how many players have moved on to play junior or college hockey, what kind of tournaments they are going to play in, how many games. Discuss team philosophy; do they promote their players with scouting packages? Find out about their dry land program. Do they have a sports psychologist? Who will be the billet? How many practices per week? All these little details will help you find the best situation for your player to develop in.

You as a parent are certainly entitled to get all the information and make sure that you are comfortable with the program before you commit.

This is also the formula to your minor hockey program. During the rep tryout, or parent meeting, find out the details, go over them with your child at home, and together make the decision. Once you have made the decision to play on the team you have chosen, that is when we as parents need to change roles, from parents to supportive bystanders, watching your child develop through the season on his own. If he is having a problem, guide him, and help him become confident enough to come to the coach himself, and try to resolve any issue. But you as the parent need to stay in the background and let him grow as a person. Trust me he will get more respect from the coach and he will continue to learn many valuable lessons.

The one thing I do know as a coach and interviewing hundreds of coaches at various levels is the worst thing that a player can ever be labeled as, and no fault of his own is **a kid that has a medaling parent**. I have seen a lot of players let go that were good enough to make the team, but the coaches didn't want to deal with the baggage that comes with the player, that is the parent. Do your research ask questions, gather information, make the decision, then get out of the way and let him thrive!

HOCKEY DEVELOPMENT CAMPS

CHAPTER II
PLAYER AND PARENT SUCCESS, THE MARSH FAMILY

S hane Marsh wanted to be a goalie ever since he can remember, he and his dad used to play outside in the yard for hours on end, not much different than thousands of other families, but this is where Shane's story, differs from most other players.

Shane played House hockey up until his second year of Bantam. Not because he wasn't good enough to play rep, but the fact that Shane grew up in a town that had several goalies that were also very good, Shane tried out for the rep team, and year after year he was let go to play on the house team.

What made Shane so special is that every time he got cut; Shane would go home, regroup and be more motivated than ever to make the next team he would try out for. His dad, Gerry, would also feel the disappointment from Shane's lack of success, but success cannot always be measured by making the team. In my mind, success is being able to handle any situation, good or bad. Shane's father knew that playing hockey at the highest level was important to Shane, which then made it very important to his father.

Gerry would go home and regroup, and then do everything possible to help his son achieve his goal of playing hockey at the highest level possible. He never blamed the coaches, or the players that were involved.

As a second year Bantam, and after having a very good tryout camp, Shane was once again released to play Bantam house. But this time Shane caught a bit of a break. The Midget Rep team in town had only one goalie. The coach of the midget team saw the determination and skill that this young man had, and offered him a spot on the Midget team as their backup goalie. Shane jumped at the chance. He then went on to have his most productive year as a goalie, playing in several games and proving to everyone that he was a very sound technical goalie. When I asked Shane If he felt he had something to prove to himself as well as the others, his answer was a resounding why? I always believed in my heart that I was a quality goalie and when I got the chance, I would be ready to make the most of it. This young man I could tell was much more mature than his tender age of 14.

The following year Shane was once again faced with disappointment as he was released from the Midget rep team he had just played the previous year for. The problem was that there were now too many goalies at the midget level, and Shane was again the odd man out. Being released didn't shake Shane's confidence, he was more determined than ever. But he still reluctantly was forced to go down to play on the Midget house.

This was a unique year in Summerland, they had just received approval to have a Junior B franchise in their community and I was fortunate enough to be named the team's 1st head coach GM. I had watched Shane play for several years, and would have loved to recruit him onto my team. Shane came out to the tryouts and was defiantly a very capable goalie that would be an asset to our team. But unfortunately we ran into some unforeseen road blocks trying to affiliate him to our team. Since Shane was not a carded rep player, we could not have him come up and play any games.

When I met with Shane I told him he could practice with us, but could not be entered into any games. I could see the disappointment in his eyes, but again like a true competitor, he shook my hand and said he would love to be part of this team even if he couldn't play any games, so he practiced with the junior team and played his games on the house team.

The following season Shane and his dad decided to go to some junior camps that were out of town, in a place where his reputation as a house goalie would not come into the equation. Shane went to the Creston Valley Thunder Cats Junior B Camp. He made that team as one of their goalies. He moved to Creston got settled in and ended up playing in three games before lightning struck again, Unfortunately for Shane, a local goalie was brought up to play on the Junior team as he had no midget team to play on. This once again left Shane looking for a place to play.

Back to Penticton Shane went for midget tryouts, but before the tryouts were complete, Shane heard about a Junior B team in Beaver Lodge that was looking for a goalie. So Shane once again was on the move with his devoted father to Beaver Lodge, about a 10 hour trip. Shane was carded immediately with Beaver Lodge, he played 2 league games, with a 1 and 1 record, but was again released when the local goalie decided to stay home and not move to play junior A like once thought. Shane at this point decided it would be best to come home and finish the year in Penticton, with the Midget AA team. All these local goalies getting in the way of his dreams must have been frustrating to say the least. Shane and his dad decided that if he had a good year back home, he would finally be able to play a full season of junior hockey. At this point I personally would have given up the dream of playing junior hockey at all, but not Shane. He always believed he would and could make it to the junior level and maybe even further. The Following season Shane was ready for camp and in the best shape of his life. He chose to tryout just down the road in Osoyoos. Shane had a tremendous camp; he made the club and played in 10 games with a very good Osoyoos hockey team. This time it was a bit more of a shock when he was released as a goalie from Osoyoos. This time another local goalie was cut from a Junior A team and wanted to come back home to play.

HOCKEY DEVELOPMENT CAMPS

This time Shane was left scratching his head, He thought for sure he had earned his spot on the team, going 6-4 in the 10 game he played. Shane had heard it all before, the coach liked him, thought he was a great goalie but circumstances has forced the team's hand, and he was being let go. This goes to show you how tough the hockey industry can be on these young kids. In my mind at this point Shane had made his best effort and had come home to decide to either go to work or to college, and hockey would take a backseat to life, boy was I wrong.

At the ripe old age of 18, Shane was again on the move with his dad to another tryout; this time in Sannach BC on Vancouver Island .Shane again made the team and was settled in committed to complete his 1st Junior B full season. This team was run differently than other Junior B teams around the province. Unlike most other junior B teams, and because of financial restraints, every player on the Saanach team was local. That is all but Shane; the difficulty with this situation was that Shane had no billet family to live with so Shane was sent home until they could rectify the billet situation. Finally Shane was called back to Saanach to begin his junior career. Shane got settled in and felt at home right away, he was very happy with his new billet family. Shane was finally on his way! After 8 league games and after Shane really started feeling this was going to be the year. It happened again, Shane was sent back home. This time not because the team didn't want him, but because the team decided that they didn't have the money to pay the billet fees. They also didn't want to start the trend of paying to billet players in their organization as they were concerned that it would become expected. This excuse was different than the previous ones, but either way you slice it, Shane was again out of a place to play. On his long drive home Shane was diverted to a junior team in Cold Lake Alberta, who was in desperate need of a goaltender. Shane didn't hesitate; Cold Lake had Billeting and an immediate home to go to. So Shane, with his dads support detoured to Cold Lake Alberta. He was immediately carded and played in 23 more games finishing his first year of Junior B hockey at the age of 19.

Most hockey people say if you are not playing junior hockey by the age of 16 or 17, well then you just should forget the thought of a hockey Scholarship, or playing any sort of pro hockey at all. This is completely false, of course it would be easier to make it to the junior level at an early age, but remember that everyone develops athletically, physically, and mentally at different times. Players may not be ready to leave home, or want to graduate at home before thinking of playing junior hockey, and that is ok.

Any Scout can recognize a young all star player, they are easy to identify. The dedicated scouts take pride in finding that player that people may have overlooked, the players that need those extra few years to develop, good character kids. All the scouts I met with talk about those players they found either in a remote area, or that started junior hockey late in their careers, players that were overlooked by other scouts.

The following year Shane went to Thunder Bay for his 1st Junior A Main camp tryout. He was a long way from home, and again Shane made the original Roster. This time Shane decided on his own to come back home, this decision is one that I still think today Shane regrets. Shane decided instead to go to college, a decision I found out later was a move that will change his career path forever. After coming home, Shane found out that he was too late to enroll in college and tryout for the team in Redeer Alberta. Shane ended up playing the rest of the season for the Pinoka Stampeders in the HJHL junior B league, awaiting a chance to play the next year at the college level.

The next Season Shane cracked the line up at Briercrest College, the team played in the ACAC, a league full of ex CHL Players and several professional players, a great league that was well respected throughout the Country. Shane's first season was a good one; it was just an honor to be there. The next year all Shane's hard work and dedication, family support and simply not giving up flourished. Shane earned his way becoming the Starting Goalie at the College level. That year Shane played in every game and was voted **1st Team All Conference**, an award that is decided by all the coaches in the league. This was a very prestigious and deserving award for him to receive. Shane and his family had finally gotten the respect that he so richly deserved.

It goes to show you that with sheer determination, the right attitude, proper family support and guidance you can have success at anything if you just simply believe in yourself. Shane is currently entering his last year at Briercrest College where he will be finishing his degree. I do not know what Shane will do next with his hockey future? But I do know that whatever path he takes, HE WILL BE SUCCESSFUL!

CHAPTER 12
LIFE IS A COMPETITION, LIFE SKILLS LEARNED THROUGH HOCKEY

Parents always wonder about the future for their children, are they good enough academically are they fully prepared for the real world out there once they leave the nest? Will they be successful at their chosen line of work? Are they going to be healthy well adjusted adults? All of these concerns are valid and very important to each and every one of us.

Have you ever thought about the intangibles that sport teaches all of us as amateur athletes? Rep Hockey and higher is and will continue to be a world that is based strictly on performance, ability to play under pressure plus individual and team success.

Whether it be the team, or the players and coaches, they fall under the same microscope, if you are winning, all is well with the world, if you are losing, you a subject to individual and team criticism. At the Minor hockey levels, it comes from you guessed it, the parents; they are the biggest babies in the world when things are not going well with their particular team they are involved with. The coach doesn't know what he is doing, or certain players should not be on the team, goalie is no good, and the list goes on and on. When the team isn't performing to its so called potential guess who is taking most of the ridicule, warranted or not, the coach. I understand, as a coach myself we do need to be accountable to the parents to a certain degree. But I have come to the realization that coaches will never be able to totally please every player and parent, on each individual team. Coaches must continue to try to only please the team as a whole, and forget about the petty parents that are going to complain no matter what you do.

Remember, your sons and daughters also take on a lot of the pressure to have team success, and dealing with this pressure is a very important part of your young athlete's mental development. Individual and team pressure is not all bad because it relates to real life in so many ways. Our jobs are all associated with pressure whether it is to close a sale, to meet a deadline, to deal with employees or to just be courteous to a customer; we All will need to deal with many stressful situations in our lifetime. I believe that these pressures in minor hockey if handled correctly, will help our children develop skills that will be beneficial throughout their lifetime. Hockey and life relate and intertwine in so many ways it is mind boggling, we also form some of our closest friendships plus tend to lead very healthy and productive academic careers.

To be a good at any given sport, and keep your school marks up, takes great discipline and excellent time management. Parents again you can be a tremendous help by making your athlete be accountable for his actions at an early age, make sure his homework is done and his marks in school stay the same, not higher marks, but make sure as the hockey intensifies, so does the homework to keep him on task, as being a good student is as important as being a quality player.

Do not let any scout, GM of a team or coach, tell you that your student athlete will be able to catch up in school at a later date, or let your son convince you that he needs more time to practice, or work out. Just help him manage his time more wisely if it is important to him, between the 2 of you it can be worked out.

Hockey also teaches players work ethic, commitment, and How to succeed as a team. Athletes will deal with personal conflict on many bases, players don't always like each other but they must work together for the betterment of the team. These are all skills that will be very beneficial in your own personal development. So don't be upset if your son doesn't make the NHL, or the junior leagues for that matter, remember how many real important life skills your child will take with them just participating in the sport.

As the Coordinator of the International Development Tournament in Penticton BC Canada, I was fortunate enough to listen to several very high profile people speak at our tournament end banquet, Wayne Flemming, assistant coach with team Canada in 2002 Olympics, gold medalists. Mike Barnett, Wayne Gretsky's agent and GM of the Phoenix Coyotes. BOB Nicholson Hockey Canada President, Barry Smith Vancouver Canucks Assistant Coach, Dan Heatly current player with the Ottawa Senators, all these professionals were great speakers, but one special individual came to mind that sums up this chapter. The Founder of the Okanagan Hockey School, Larry Lund. Larry is first and foremost a very caring honest family man, his success with OHS and the Okanagan Hockey Academy was no fluke. Larry was a member of the Houston Aeros; Avco World Trophy Champions. He also represented the Aeros on the Western Division team in the WHA All-Star game for two seasons. Larry is a great teacher of the fundamentals of the game, his passion to give back to the hockey world is unparalleled to this date, which leads me to a speech that Larry gave at one of our International Development Tournament banquets. Larry is a very big advocate of academics in conjunction with athletics. The speech he delivered at our IDT Banquet, in 2005 was the most powerful inspirational speeches I was fortunate enough to take in. Larry spoke about school as he always does, but then he made reference to a personal experience he had with his son Eric.

I believe that Eric like all others had the dream of playing hockey like his dad did making a career out of it. But like so many other players, Eric finished his hockey career at the minor hockey level, playing midget AAA in Penticton BC as his highest level. Eric was a motivated young man and decided to pursue his career in School where he became a lawyer some 7 years later.

This is where Mr. Lund's story relates to all hockey players and parents in such a positive way. Eric applied to a prestigious law firm in New York; he was short listed down to 10 applicants out of hundreds, an honor just to get that far. Eric was finally successful in getting the position after further interviews of the final applicants. After several months at his new dream job, Eric finally asked his boss, what was it that made him the individual chosen over all the other very qualified applicants. His boss said to Eric, that going through your application one last time, I seen that you played hockey, a very intense competitive sport, and I knew then you would bring that same intensity and desire to our firm, that is one of the reason we chose you over the others. I'm sure it didn't hurt that Eric was also an excellent Student and of course Lawyer, but it goes to show you that no matter how far you take your hockey Career that it can help put you above others as being a competitive person by nature. Hockey no matter how far you go in the sport is a excellent way of life as a youth athlete and it will help teach you discipline, commitment and how to deal with winning and losing as a team and a person. So you parents out there that think your son or daughter is not going to the NHL, don't fret, you are teaching your child some very good life skills that will come in handy during the course of their lives.

CHAPTER 13
INTIMIDATION AND FIGHTING, LEARNING TO PLAY FEARLESS

Hockey is one of the most emotional sports around the globe, it is very physical and intense and at times out of control. A quality hockey player plays on the edge, and learns not to cross over the line. As there is a fine line between being an effective competitive player, or becoming a player that lives in the penalty box and can't control his emotions. Fighting is a production of these high emotions and whether you like it or not, it is and will continue to be a big part of the game.

If you as a player can achieve any advantage over another player, it puts you at a decided advantage. If you are afraid to go into the corner and compete for loose pucks or you are even hesitant about going into the corner, you will not have the success that you want. Pure and simple hockey players must be both mentally and physically.

This does not mean you need to be huge in size, it helps but it is not the only consideration. If you are a smaller player, the same principal applies you must try to be the 1st guy to the puck, but you also must play smarter, you may not be able to go in and outmuscle a larger defenseman, but you can outthink him, be evasive, do not get into a position where you can get hurt, get in tight to the wall as quick as possible, then if you are checked, all he can do is squish you along the boards. Keep your head on a swivel, and be aware at all times, but you must be willing to go into the tough areas of the ice, the corners, the slot zone, and in front of the net. As a young hockey player, this is a trait you either have or you don't, and parents, you cannot just make your kid fearless. I your player is timid at an early age don't worry, I have seen players come out of there shell up to the age of 17. I refer again to the concept that playing fearless hockey happens directly by playing there minor hockey, at the appropriate skill level. If you continue to have your son play at the highest level, maybe a level that he is not totally comfortable with he may not get that confidence to play the game at his personal best.

As the players get older and more intense, fighting becomes the next intimidation obstacle in there hockey careers. This experience does separate the men from the boys. This does not mean that you have to fight, although it does usually happen at some point for most players. When fighting is allowed in the game at the junior level, some players are very uptight and can't play their game as they have in the past, driving the net hard, first into the corners, laying out that big hit, because in the back of their mind is will he want to kick my but, or will one of his teammates want to do so. For players that are in this situation they need to realize that fighting is not as scary as it seems, and that you most nights will not need to be involved in these altercations. Once you decide to make the jump to junior hockey, as a player going to camp, you must be able to play fearless and not back down from any situation.

If you are challenged to a fight you need to engage, but you 1st need the tools to understand how to show up to answer the bell, and not be vulnerable to getting your clock cleaned. Put quite bluntly, if someone makes up his mind that he's going to fight you, you can't just hold on and hope for the best. You have to punch back or be able to get close quickly. It's not about pride, it's not about the respect of your teammates ... it's about survival.

When a player is confronted with a fighting situation, not the standard pushing and shoving in front of the net. I'm talking about when an opponent jumps on you for shooting the puck after the whistle, or for giving his goalie a love-tap in the crease. Every player should be prepared for any on-ice situation, and like it or not, this does include fighting. Below are a set of hockey fight survival guidelines.

Follow these suggestions, and be confident, you will do fine in your first altercation. Once the 1st one is over, trust me you will realize that you can take care of yourself, and you and your game will continue to develop. Fighting is not in any way encouraged, but it is a part of the game.

Stay on your feet and challenge. The first thing you might say is, "I don't want to get thrown out of the game." But "challenging" doesn't necessarily mean "fighting" with your opponent. If you are in a fight, you will get kicked out, unless you go on your hands and knees and turtle, which is even more dangerous than fighting because who knows what the guy on top is going to do. You have to stay on your feet. And if you stand, you will more than likely get tossed out of the game. So make the best of it and be prepared.

Be in good condition. This statement is so very true, but the most tiring 30 seconds you will ever spend in any sport is hockey fighting. The mixture of trying to avoid punches, landing punches and keeping your balance on an 1/8-inch blade of steel will get you tired.

Have a tight-fitting helmet

Make sure your helmet fits snug and use all the straps for the cage or visor. This should be elementary, but a lot of players like to just pop their hockey hat on and go. If your helmet is too loose, or if you are not using all of the cage and chin straps, two things can happen. One, the helmet could fly off, leaving your head unprotected. Two, the helmet can get jostled around and impede your vision. It is very difficult to defend yourself when a cage is flying up in front of your face. Keep all the straps on tight to avoid this situation.

Helmets on or off?

The worst thing about being in a fight with a player that has his helmet on is that you run the chance of breaking your hand or fingers by striking the helmet with your bare knuckles.

Another thing, don't ever take your own helmet off to try to show your bravery before a fight unless it is required by the league, which is the usual in Canadian junior hockey, but be very aware of the league rules you are playing in. If you are a young player, you probably have not fought on skates before so be aware of who your opponent is, all it takes is one solid punch from that overgrown 200-pound player who is already shaving to break your nose. So always be aware who you are battling with , if he is a known fighter, you know if a fight breaks out with you and him, you will want to get in close and hang on, throwing short punches until the officials break it up. Don't let him get lose and throw hay makers because chances are you may get your clock cleaned, if you stay in close, the big guys will have a tough time getting in any hard effective punches. Just dropping the gloves with a bigger opponent will be a victory win or lose. Always remember you need to be aware of your opponent, is he at the end of a shift and maybe a little bit tired giving you an advantage if you are fresh. BE AWARE Here are some tips regarding fighting, and how you can prepare for that inevitable battle.

Use basic fighting mechanics

Don't keep your feet parallel. Pick a side and stick with it. Lead with the right or the left, and don't face your opponent head on and get in early.

Practice your balance

After practice, ask your coach if you can work on a balance drill. He may not think it's a good idea and tell you to get off the ice, but if you have a few minutes while the Zamboni is getting warmed up, grab a buddy (be sure to tell him what you are doing first, you're both teammates, eh?) and through pushing and pulling, try to knock the other of his/her feet.

Leave it on the ice

Finally, leave it on the ice. Don't continue your scrum in the hallway, or parking lot. That is when fighting can get scary. It is a controlled environment while players are on the ice; off the ice, others can get involved or there is no official to protect the integrity of the fight. Hockey fights are hockey fights, it's nothing personal. There are no guns, no knives on the ice. It's just two players blowing off steam in the heat of the battle.

Do I need to fight to make it to Junior Hockey

This question is very simple. "No" does it help to show that you are a player that is not afraid to stick up for a teammate or not afraid to compete in the corners. The answer then would be "Yes"; players that end up in altercations are sometimes a problem for team, as you can end up on the penalty kill far more often than you may want. So remember there is a fine line between sticking up for yourself and being a distraction on your team.

Fighting during training camps just shows that you are not afraid of competing in any situation, this also does get you noticed just for the fact that you and your opponent are the only 2 people the evaluators are watching as the play has been stopped because of the altercation

Coaches all say there is to be no fighting in camp, but in almost all cases, it is just lip service. The odd fight during a spirited game, just adds fuel to the game. The coaches all like fights, don't kid yourself; it is part of the game. It is also an easy measuring stick to see if the player will do anything to make the team, is he a fearless player.

This is not meant to detour players from the way they approach the game, it is just the truth. Something to remember, if you can play the game with no fear, not afraid of finishing that check in the corner with passion, and not afraid of battling in front of the net for position, with no concerns that the player that you are competing with may want to drop his gloves and fight, you still can have great success as a player.

What the coaches are looking for are players that are not afraid to play in the dirty areas of the ice, and players that will not be intimidated by anyone. They are not looking for fighters, but fighting is an easy way to show that you are an aggressive, fearless player.

CHAPTER 14
YOGA FOR HOCKEY PLAYERS?

Not only is Yoga a powerful tool for stretching and strengthening the muscles plus increasing flexibility. It is also offers a comprehensive way of increasing concentration and maximizing breathing techniques. Keeping yourself in tune with every aspect of your own body. From your skeletal and muscular makeup to breathing and thought patterns. Through Yoga you will not only feel better, but you will find that your workouts are much more productive as well as feeling better with less muscle fatigue and stiffness.

Working with the Hockey Academy we would have the players go through regular Yoga sessions throughout the season. Since hockey has changed so much the last 10 or 15 years we are continually looking to gain the advantage over other players. Gone are the days that your summers were time to relax until the next season. Today's hockey players are continuously trying to get stronger and bigger during the off season. Yoga the past few years has become a staple among the serious hockey player or any athlete for that matter.

Working with a professional Yoga instructor, Darren Wilms a 210 lb ex football player sure opened my player's eyes last year. When we decided to put Yoga into our routine at the Bantam Rep level, it was met with a little resistance as the players thought Yoga was a routine for girls, not big tough hockey players. But after Darren put them through a simple Yoga work out and gave them the understanding on how this could not only help them physically, but it could help them with injury prevention and being able to recover from an injury much sooner, it became a hit.

It also didn't hurt for my players to see Darren as he went through the routine, he is very flexible and the kids were very impressed by not only his size and strength, but his coordination, balance and flexibility. If you look around every community has qualified Yoga instructors, and they are not very expensive .You can either join a class or have your whole team work with an instructor. Either way it will help your team build strength and confidence. What you will discoverer through Yoga is the ability and knowledge to maximize your warm ups, and cool downs, it ultimately enhances your fitness, and increase your focus. Many people think that Yoga is all about meditation or all about stretching or all about chanting. What Yoga is about is being aware of yourself: both mentally and physically. And for any athlete, this can only be an asset. It is up to you which type of Yoga you choose to practice and decide the elements of Yoga that suits your personal needs.

As a hockey player, it is important to maintain muscular balance especially since the game naturally favors the weak areas of the body. We are prone to stiffness in the lower back, tight quads, hip flexors, and hamstrings. Yoga offers: hundreds of comprehensive stretches which align the spine, warm up exercises which activate all of the muscles in the body, and postures which target specific muscle groups. It naturally stretches and strengthens the back muscles, opens up the hips and increases flexibility in the legs.

Through Yoga a hockey player can become more aware of muscle imbalances and how to strengthen these muscles in order to prevent injuries. Yoga can also be used in rehabilitation to build up strength when coming off an injury: since each posture is only as intense as the athlete allows it to be, you can gently ease your body back to full health. Yoga also sharpens the mind and since concentration and focus are a vital part of hockey, it cannot help but increase your game awareness. If your team doesn't believe in using Yoga, go out yourself and get some personal instruction Final Yoga puts you in touch with your breathing. Breathing control is essential for peak game performance to ensure oxygen is being delivered to the muscles. This decreases the likelihood of cramping and helps neutralize lactic acids which also will help you be able to perform at the highest level.

Yoga has gradually become accepted in the sports industry as a valuable and essential part of the training program for many athletes around the world. Don't be left behind, find a Yoga instructor and get started. It doesn't matter your age or ability, this is a skill that you can keep using for a lifetime.

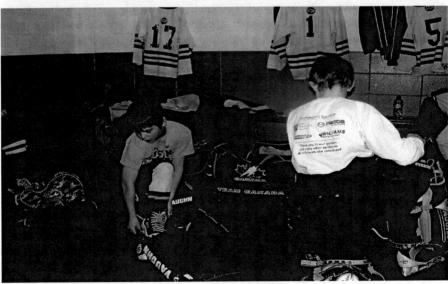

HOCKEY DEVELOPMENT CAMPS

CHAPTER 15
HOCKEY TRAINING, WORKING WITH YOUR CHILD AT HOME

When Wayne Gretsky was asked years ago in his prime, What was the one thing that young Canadian hockey players are missing in their game? The answer was, individual creativity. Where do you think the players develop their creative side? It was at home playing road hockey, shooting on an empty net, stick handling with a tennis ball. All these skills are developed at home without parent or coaches supervision. Kids are very creative by nature. Give them a hockey stick and a ball, and they are ready to invent new games and develop new skills without even knowing it. Tennis balls or even golf balls are just fine for the backyard game or in your home on the floor in front of the TV, watching Hockey Night in Canada, emulating some of the moves performed by the players.

If your child shows that he loves working on his game at home, you may want to invest into a Hockey specific type ball. The best one out there for your money is the Swedish Stick handling ball. About 15 years ago North American hockey players started to copy the Swedish players who used wooden balls to practice their stick handling. The North American players did not have access to the wooden balls so they began using golf balls instead. Many College and NHL Players who have been using a golf ball say that they prefer using the wooden balls because they do not bounce as much as the golf ball and you can shoot the wooden balls. These balls coast around $15 each, and will last forever if they are not lost. This unique training aid is fairly simple and measures 2 inches in diameter. The wood is amazingly durable and can be used on all but the roughest surfaces, it is most effective on wood, tile, smooth concrete, or even carpeted surfaces. This ball is primarily used for developing soft and quick hands, better hand eye coordination, and confidence. Use this ball 10-15 minutes a day and you will see a dramatic improvement in your child's ability to handle the puck.

Another tool that can be used at home and is very effective for balance and stick handling is a Wobble Board, or rocker board. These pieces of equipment are also durable and can be used anywhere. Stick handling off-ice with a wobble board is considered one of the best ways to improve your puck skills, while developing balance, coordination and a stronger core. This exercise is practiced in all the top hockey schools and training centers throughout the world, and the great thing about it is that you can easily do this at home and get the same results. Another easy to use devise is something called the tape to tape passing center. It is a 6 or 8 ft surface area with an elastic band system at the end of the surface. When you pass the puck down the surface, the puck rebounds right back at you and you can now practice passing and receiving a pass all by yourself.

This is a great time for a young player to work on his own, no pressure from a coach breathing down his neck or dad watching his every move. This device is less than $200 and well worth the investment especially if he doesn't have a brother or sister to play with on a regular basis. Like an actual game, the puck is constantly in motion with this system, and it gives the flexibility to practice game situations in the back yard or basement or in the living room, without the need of a partner to feed passes.

Another great source of information is a DVD set done by Sean Skinner. Sean Skinner is a stick handling expert, you will not believe how fast and soft his hands are. Sean has spent a life time bettering his skills, and he shares all his tips and drills with us. This 5 DVD set is broken up into 1) Theory & Preparation 2) Stick Agility Techniques 3) The Moves, Fakes or Dekes 4) On-Ice Drills & Drills for Coaches 5) Dry land Training for Stick handling. This is the best and absolutely most complete Stick handling DVD set available and Something I would recommend buying for any young athlete. There is also a lot of interesting ideas about training at home. Remember that watching this guy stickhandle is unbelievable, and something that may be a bit overwhelming, so make sure you take the information with a grain of salt. You will not be able to stickhandle as well as Sean right away, but the drills that he has will help you grow as a player and increase your ability to handle the puck with a greater amount of confidence.

When I was with the Okanagan Hockey School, This program was always on the cutting edge of development, the company staff as a whole would get together on a yearly basis and evaluate how the school could improve its training techniques both on and off the ice. The Skills center was second to none, and they were constantly upgrading the drills and design of the equipment used. There was of coarse several shooting stations, and an area where the player's shots were videotaped for review and analysis. The most unique stations were the ones used to develop puck handling skills and passing techniques. At home there are hundreds of stick handling drills that can be thought up of with just a few pucks and a sheet of synthetic ice. Here is a sample of some drills that you can do at home with some very simple devices. Go to your local arena and talk to their staff and ask if they have any used rink board pieces. They come in 4 by 8 sheets and one sheet will be enough to get started. The rink staff may sell it or even give you a sheet. This sheet will give you enough room to shoot and work with pucks.

Other drills can be done, put 5 pucks in a line spaced equally apart, stickhandle up and down through the pucks, you can stickhandle for hand, backhand, around your body on a Bosu ball. The possibilities are endless and they don't cost but a few dollars to start, plus no very expensive ice rentals. All these ideas and more are found in Sean Skinners DVD sets, they are worth the money.

Sean's website is an excellent source of information; he has all the gadgets and devices that you can imagine. The only reason I am referring to his expertise is that I have personally used a lot of his equipment and ideas during my time at the Okanagan Hockey School. I am encouraging all my readers to visit Sean's site and go through all the equipment and videos, then make your own decisions. www.skinnerhockey.com Remember Knowledge is power.

Before purchasing any DVD set, or equipment, first ask your local association if they have a copy before you buy them yourself .As a lot of associations may have a video library themselves. The Videos that Sean made were innovative and some of the most creative work that has ever been published. The coaches and players at the International Development Tournament always enjoyed the videos we presented to them.

The main purpose to this chapter is to inform and encourage all the parents and players that there is a wealth of knowledge out there. You owe it to yourself to tap into all the information you can and become the expert in your chosen athletic sport. The internet is a great place to start, if it is to find out information on a hockey school, or to find out how to improve your shot, this information is all available at a reasonable price. Have a look around!

CHAPTER 16
NUTRITION FOR THE YOUNG ATHLETE

O ne of the areas where I see a lot of room for major improvement is proper nutrition. It is very vital for all hockey players and especially for young growing children. Poor eating habits could actually destroy good training efforts or seriously undermine the intensity of the workouts. Improper nutritional habits and lack of knowledge could cause an athlete to run out of energy after about 30 minutes or less. One thing to remember when discussing nutrition with your child is everyone is different.

If proper nutrition could take your game to the next level, I'm sure you would want to if you were a real dedicated hockey player. Believe it or not, you can influence the way you play and the energy you play with on a regular basis by eating the right foods. Plus equally important is the time you eat pre and post game. To compete at your very best, you must treat your body like a temple. You would not put second rate fuel into your new car, because it will not perform to its full potential, your body runs on the same principle. If you eat sporadically, you will play the same way. What if an Evaluator came to see you play on a particular day, and you didn't prepare to play your best, both physically and mentally, and you had a bad game? In the evaluators eyes you could be seen as an average player. Not the impression you want to leave, and that impression will be difficult to change for that particular evaluator as Scouts must make snapshot decisions on players as they are not able to see everyone play on a regular basis, it is simply not possible. So for any dedicated athlete, don't let a day go by that you are not fully prepared to compete at your very best, because you can never tell when and who will be watching.

Everyday eating
When you don't have a practice or a game, you are refueling your body, and building up energy for the next workout, game or practice, all these activities are all approached in a slightly different way.

Carbohydrates are your fuel
Try to have 2 servings with every meal and 1 serving between meals.

Body weight/LBS	Serving Per Day
150-160 lbs	8-9 {436g}
160-170 lbs	9-10 {463g}
170-180 lbs	10-11{490g}
180-190 lbs	11-12{518g}
190-200lbs	12-13{545g}
200 plus lbs	13-14{572g}

Examples
- 1 Bagel   = 2 servings
- 1 slice of bread   = 1 serving
- 1 bowl of cereal   = 1 serving

Some really good choices are granola, vector, cornflakes, mini wheats, all without sugar added.

- 1 bowl rice pref. brown   = 2 servings
- 1 pita   = 2 servings
- 1 bowl pasta   = 2 servings
- 1 granola or cereal bar   = 1 serving
- 1 muffin   = 1 serving
- 1 baked potato   = 1 serving
- Fruit also counts as carbs, 1 piece   = 1 serving
- 1 cup 100% fruit juice   = 1 serving
- It is important to try to get at least 5 -7 servings of fruit and vegetables in your daily diet.

PROTEIN, is the building blocks for your muscles!

After any exercise, weather it being a hard workout, or a yoga session, a game, your muscles need to rebuild themselves to get ready for your next workout. Protein is also great to have for snacks to, have 1-2 servings with every meal.

Body weight, lbs	Serving/day
160-170 lbs	4-6 {154g}
170-180 lbs	5-6 {163g}
180-190 lbs	5-7 {173g}
190-200 lbs	6-8 {182g}
200 plus lbs	7-9 {191g}

Examples

Steak, Roast Beef, Chicken Breast, Lean pork Chops, Fish, these all = 1 full serving, the portion is roughly the size of you palm.

1 bowl of beans	= 1 serving
1 hand full of peanut s	= 1 serving
1 handful of trail mix	= 1 serving
½ salmon fillet	= 2 servings
1 can of tuna	= 2 servings
1 large glass of milk 2%	= 1 serving
1 protein bar	= 1 serving
1 scoop protein powder	= 1 serving

Protein shakes or fruit smoothies are a great source of protein and a great afternoon snack. Simply mix 1-2 scoops protein powder, 1 cup of milk, a cup of the fruit of your choice, 1 spoon of honey and if wanted 1 package of Nestles instant breakfast into a blender.

Mark Rycroft Recipe, A great start in the morning for the active athlete is 1 cup of cooked oatmeal, 1-2 scoops of protein powder 1 cup of 100% juice, 1 cup of frozen fruit your choice, mix in the blender, you then have a healthy start to your day, and you can take it with you on the go.

I got this Protein Shake recipe from one of the NHL players that came to our hockey school Mark Rycroft. Mark each year would come to the International Development Tournament to speak to all our players, it would always be in the morning, and as far as I can remember Mark carried this drink with him at every morning lecture. He was always asked what he was drinking and why. Mark stated that this was part of his daily routine, a similar breakfast every morning. He also pointed out that several players he plays with have a similar routine. It may not be for everybody, but it works for him. My recommendation is give this a try, be creative and find the best fruits that work for your tastes.

Hydration

Water and sports drinks used to keep your body hydrated is as important part of your everyday diet. Water is in every cell in your body. You can survive only 3-4 days with absolutely no water, so you can start to see the importance of proper hydration. When exercising, you can lose up to 2-3 liters of water by simply sweating. To keep your body functioning at its highest competitive level, you must replenish the lost fluids before you become dehydrated. If you find you are thirsty, chances are that you are already dehydrated. You should always carry a water bottle with you, just taking sips all day long. You should be able to consume at least 10 large glasses per day as an athlete. Always try to avoid caffeine, red bull, and any other quick fix energy drinks; they are simply **NOT GOOD FOR YOU**

Game day Eating

2-6 hours before the game, this is your pre game meal full of carbs and protein. Remember you will need to do some trial meals during practice time to find out what gives you personally the best consistent energy level. Do not eat any really fatty foods or foods high in sugar like chocolate bars etc. Just use common sense. Remember 1 sports drinks = 2 servings of Carbs. Once you arrive at the rink usually 1-2 hours before a game depending on the coach and the program, usually water and sports drinks are usually the best, a piece of fresh fruit or a healthy energy bar, but keep it light.

Just before the game and during the course of the game, continue to drink water, and if needed use watered down sports drinks half and half. Try to keep drinking little sips at every possible moment, this is important for staying at your peak performance during the whole game, you never know how much ice time you are going to get, or how long the game will last. Always OVER PREPARE.

After the Game

Believe it or not, what you do with your body post game, i.e. stretching, and of course replenishing your body with quality foods, and re hydrating are very important especially if you are playing again the next day.

This will help your body recover quicker and remember that time is important, you must replenish right after the game,30 minutes to 2 hours is optimum, don't wait as it can and will affect your performance the next day. Remember immediately after a game, you are already preparing for your next athletic workout, whether it is in the gym, at practice or at a game, FAILURE TO PREPARE IS PREPARING TO FAIL.

Junk Food

Having a bag of chips or a chocolate bar is ok to have in moderation, but when you are playing hockey during the season, try to stay away from so called empty foods. As you get older you will need to get more and more serious about the nutritional value you are consuming. Continue to build these strong values throughout your family, as these eating habits will help you throughout your whole life. So as a parent you can again encourage your child to make better choices. This is not only a good way to live, but you will be healthier and more energetic no matter how far your child goes in the game of hockey. As you can see, hockey isn't just about strapping on the gear and going to play and have fun. The one thing that we as parents can control, without being deceitful is in order for you to play hockey, or any sport for that matter, you must put all the nutritional pieces together, and become sort of an expert on your own body. As I stated at the beginning of the chapter everyone is different, you must experiment and find out what works best for you. Parents, you can guide your child, but let the athlete make the decisions, as he knows his body best.

CHAPTER 17
MENTAL TOUGHNESS

In this chapter I am not going to give you advise regarding the how to, but what I will do is go through my experience, plus give you some insight working with the Okanagan Hockey School and the Okanagan Hockey Academy . Detailing how very important the mind is to not only your game, but again parents it spreads into everyday life. This is just another aspect of not only giving your child every chance to succeed at their chosen sport, but to also better prepares them to have success at life.

We will start at the players early ages of development. John Lee Kootnikoff is a motivational speaker. I have sat through many of his seminars, working with players at the ages of 8 through 17.

The message was always the same. Visualization is a very powerful tool that can and should be used prior to your athletic endeavor. John Lee would use key words like confidence, commitment, mental imagery, believe in yourself and you can achieve anything you set your heart to. All positive phrases are very powerful if you can just tap into them and believe that they will help you. The most powerful quote that I have heard and it rings true in everything you do in life is, **WHETHER YOU SAY YOU CAN OR CAN'T, YOU'RE RIGHT**. Believing that you can do something is the most important part. Mental Imagery is visualizing events before they happen, where you are in total control of the outcome. Just before a big game, you visualize yourself executing every shift to perfection. You are in total control, you see yourself if you are a defenseman, angling that player to the corner, making great outlet passes from your own end, playing the one on ones to perfection, no one is going to get buy you today. You are a goalie, you are playing the puck perfectly, you are unbeatable, and the puck seems to be as big as a beach ball. You are in the zone, today, you are the best. These are all positive feelings that can help you each and every time you go onto the ice

Dr. Saul Miller is one of North America's leading sport psychologists. He has consulted with teams in the NFL, NHL, Major League Baseball, NBA, CFL, European elite sport, plus PGA Tour golfers, as well as Olympic and national team athletes and teams in over a dozen different sports. Dr Millers Seminars with the Okanagan Hockey Academy were spectacular to say the least, Saul spoke on what he would continue to refer to is **"your TV set" which is your mind**, and how we are all ultimately in control of our own TV sets, if we don't like what we are thinking, simply change the channel. You are the boss, it is your TV. Saul told our players there are 2 common emotions, **love and fear**, his message was, you can play the game good with fear, but with the fear emotion we tend to contract, and prepare to defend ourselves. But when we love what we are doing, and are confident we can play the game GREAT! This is again a message to all the parents that we cannot make our children love the sport; we can only support them in the way they decide to play the sport, you can't make them more aggressive, and tougher.

HOCKEY DEVELOPMENT CAMPS

To do the best for your child, just be supportive, help them with positive reinforcement. Giving them the knowledge of what they can do to be successful, what you must not do is make them play the game if there heart is not into it.

I have seen it literally hundreds of times. The player is doing well at hockey, or any sport for that matter, and then your child decides that he or she is not interested in perusing the sport to the next level as you expect. You know who takes it the hardest? Of course it is most devastating to the parents, who have put in so much time and effort getting your child ready to succeed. Remember, it is your child that is playing the game, and it is there decision on how far they want to pursue the sport, but always remember during the short time your child was playing, you have better prepared your child to succeed in life. Always remember that and stop thinking of yourself, because you had your chance when you were young.

Saul would also make reference to key topics like, Leadership, Teamwork, Why teams win, Self-image, Performing under pressure. These topics Dr Miller covers in depth during his powerful lectures. I am not the expert in this field, I have just been fortunate enough to be able to sit in with Dr Saul miller, during his discussions with the team I was coaching at that time. I will tell you this, if you ever get a chance to take in one of his seminars, make sure you go. They were spectacular discussions, and make complete sense. I also was fortunate enough to spend some one on one time with Dr Miller; he was able to help me personally with several issues. Saul was very instrumental in my decision to write this book. I encourage you to read it yourself as it is very informative. Get the books; you will be happy you did.

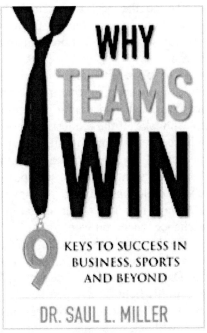

These two books will help you with not only your chosen sport, but with all the obstacles that you will encounter in everyday life.

CHAPTER 18
HOCKEY TRAINING, PRE AND POST SEASON

T he good old days are defiantly gone where getting ready for the season is just showing up for camp and working your fitness to an acceptable level there. In today's game, players are constantly looking to get quicker, stronger and have better overall cardiovascular condition. Athletics in general have defiantly become much more scientific. Hockey players are much more in tune with their bodies, and the mechanics of the sport they are playing. Being in great shape not only helps the body sustain excellence; but it is also proven that the body heals quicker.

The other main reason that players and trainers want their athletes in such great condition is simply injury prevention, having good flexibility and great core strength helps with the prevention of groin, back, and several other hockey related injuries. Here are some specific hockey training ideas and suggestions.

- You must sprint for speed
- You must run to prevent injury
- You must do agility /mobility drills to be quick and have strength
- Hockey Training tips to remember- long, slow jogging/roller blading must be kept to a minimum. Roller blading does not help you with your skating stride so it may not be the best exercise for your training routine.
- You must be flexible and be able to work on your flexibility each and every day.
- You must train your core (meaning your Abs, sides, hips, and lower back everyday
- Biking is good for long intervals, and long workouts, but it is not the greatest for speed. You can end up with back problems especially if you are not using a properly fitted bicycle.

These are the basic theories that are used for the Hockey specific athlete. The Academy I worked with had a Special trainer come in at the beginning of each season and go through our workouts and train our athletic staff how to administer his program. Remember every trainer is different and every player is also of different needs, one player may need stronger legs, where one player may be just working on quickness, or may want to shed a few pounds before his training camp. So always remember that these are strictly guidelines and they may not be exactly what your child may need. Always leave it up to the experts to make those decisions.

One thing that is for sure, you can always no matter the age, work on your flexibility daily, it is only a 10-15 minute routine and you can do it in front of the TV. Remember

FLEXIBILITY CAN BE IMPROVED EVERY DAY....

STRENGTH CAN BE IMPROVED WEEK TO WEEK.

SPEED CAN BE IMPROVED MONTH TO MONTH, THAT IS WHY YOU SHOULD WORK ON THESE CONCEPTS EVERY DAY AND EVERY WEEK. SPEED, AGILITY AND FITNESS WILL ULTIMATELY SEPARATE PLAYERS.

As athletes, you should always be in endless pursuit of greater functional strength and speed, knowing that this edge in your personal ability will lead you closer to achieving your ultimate goals. You must be committed to train for many years not weeks or months in order to develop and refine your personal technique in order to attain the strength, agility, flexibility, and speed required to reach your full potential as an athlete. With all this information, I know it can be confusing. All these technical words and concepts being thrown at you. But as a parent, you always need to do your homework, take the concepts and consult your local professional to get a program that suits your athlete's needs. The training facility that you are able to work in will dictate how and what you can do. Again all these skills that your child is learning are life skills, something that they will be able to take with them for the rest of their lives. Whatever you do, make sure your child is taught the proper technique. Lifting without proper posture or understanding of the exercise can lead to severe injury, As a parent you can give your child all the information and encourage them to start doing the things that are proven to help them develop the skills needed to improve, but ultimately the player must have the dedication and want to do it for themselves.

HOCKEY DEVELOPMENT CAMPS

It will never be you that makes your player great. You can give him the information and the understanding of what it will take to even have a chance to fulfill his potential as a complete hockey player. The one thing that parents do not understand, it is not about you, and your desires for him to play in the NHL, it is strictly your child, No matter what you say or do, or what you have done in the past as a hockey player or athlete for that matter, you can't will him, or bully him into having the desire to do all the Yoga, workouts, strength training etc to reach his full potential as a player. Sure you think you can, you can enroll him and make him go and he will, but not for him, it will be to please you. This is not the   healthy situation that you want your child in, so again, do your homework before you get your child involved, make sure he or she is doing it for the right reasons, with no pressure from the family. Your time is over and you must not try to live your dreams through your child. Again knowledge is power and all you can do is to give him the information and support his decisions, even if they are not what you want to hear. You child may just want to play with his friends in a house league, and THAT'S OK, your child will still learn all of the life skills that are taught in sport. Remember, **YOU CAN LEAD A HORSE TO WATER; BUT YOU CAN'T MAKE HIM DRINK**

(HAPT€R 19
DAR€ TO DR€AM

All players especially Canadian players all dream of one day playing in the NHL, and realistically 99.9 percent of all players do not make it. But even with the odds stacked against all of these players, we still believe we will be the one that makes the giant leap to the show.

Dealing with young players at the International Development Tournament, I found out that almost every player has the dream of playing in the NHL, only a small handful of players said they didn't want to play in the NHL and I think it was just because they were told the dream was all but impossible. I found this answer interesting so I did some investigating by speaking with the parents of those children and then again with the players themselves.

I came to the realization that the children all really wanted to play in the NHL, but through their parents, and past coaches, the kids I interviewed were basically told that they were not going to make it to the NHL, so don't get your hopes up. We all know that most players will not make it to their ultimate dream of one day playing in the NHL. But why discourage or even mention that the odds are stacked against them. Let them dream, encourage them to chase that star, and never give up. Someone has to make it, so why not your child? Who decides which players are going to move on; these are questions that we can't answer. It doesn't matter your size as several smaller players have gone on to have great NHL careers, it isn't the age you start playing the game, as players that played in the NHL have joined hockey as late as 14 years old. It is not where you come from or how much training or money your family has, as all these situations have been proven wrong on several occasions with players coming from small towns, diverse backgrounds. The one common denominator on these NHL players is they have a real passion for the game and they have not made any excuses not to succeed. So don't discourage your son or daughter to follow their dreams, because it is attainable if you just believe in yourself.

Sports are really "Preparation for Life"

Not everything we do in life is a pleasant experience. Not everything we do is beneficial. Not everything is productive. Not everything is a nurturing, loving experience. Life is full of negative, destructive experiences. Rejection, defeat and failure surround all of us. The trick is to be prepared to deal with this side of life and learn to overcome discouragement and failure. I have always felt that the great value of Hockey as a sport is that it prepares one for life. The total Athletic experience is made up of people, attitudes, beliefs, work habits, fitness, health, winning and losing, and so much more. Hockey is a cross section of lifetime experiences. It can provide so many learning situations. An athlete learns to deal with pressure and stress, sometimes self-imposed, sometimes applied by others. One learns to deal with success and failure. One learns teamwork and discipline. Hockey is a self-achievement activity with team goals and aspirations at the forefront. You can ultimately only control what you do on the ice, your work ethic and discipline is your responsibility.

The responsibility for performance ultimately lies with the individual. How well the individual has prepared physically and mentally to a large degree will determine the performance level. Many hockey players' experiences can be of the disruptive discouraging type usually with a parent leading the way. But at least a young player usually learns that this is part of life, and the athlete must learn to cope. By learning how to handle frustration and disappointment, the young Athlete gains confidence, dealing with adverse situations can and do make us more rounded complete people. The Athlete also learns dedication and commitment; these are the main foundation of any successful athlete.

Through perseverance, an athlete learns to overcome adversity. All of these experiences tend to develop an individual who is better able to handle life's hardships and face problems. As coaches and parents, we tend to preach that hard work will lead to victory. We preach that clean living and proper training such as diet, sleep and regular attendance at practices workouts and games will lead to winning. Though in the long run for a productive successful life, these are probably truthful concepts that don't always work in short term situations.

We have all been in situations where a bigger, more gifted person with poor work habits is the victor tryout after tryout. Or we've known others who never seem to study, yet get good grades. We've known business people who never seem to lift a finger, yet for one reason or another, they close deal after deal. These things just are not fair. Yet this is one of the valuable lessons that athletes learn: "Life is not fair."We don't all start out in life with the same physical, mental, emotional and financial resources. In that respect, "Life is not fair." An athlete must learn what is fair for one is not necessarily fair for another. An athlete learns we are all different and each individual controls his or her own destiny. A knowledgeable hockey player, learns to emphasize given talents and skills, and knows to attack his weaknesses which will help them improve on a regular basis. By not setting limits and restrictions, this Improvement will surely lead to success. A complete Hockey player learns if he or she does their best, then there are no failures.

An athlete learns to set realistic goals. Once a goal is reached, then new goals must be established. A Hockey Player learns that effort becomes an individual crusade. If the ultimate goal is to win the Stanley cup or even win a local tournament, then with the proper talent, dedication, belief and support, all your teammates believe it can be done. This is the positive achievement side of Hockey that I like so much. Through experience in hockey or any athletics, our young people learn attitudes and habits that will remain with them throughout the rest of their life. Most Athletes learn to be "can do" people.

Generally, these positive attitudes, belief in self and solid work habits will produce a productive adult. These former athletes enrich our society and our world, as they become adults. Because of their training, they handle life with a smile. They contribute time and energy to others in very different and positive ways. So whatever sport your child partakes in always be supportive and remember knowledge is power and how you conduct yourself at athletic events or how you handle all the disappointments and achievements that your child goes through, always remember that this experience will be part of the blueprint that will one day see your child grow into a positive part of our society, and ultimately you hold all of the cards, obtain all the knowledge to support your athlete and be there to celebrate the positive experiences and there to help them go through the tough times. Hockey is the best sport in the world, yes it is tough and demanding, and yes it is unfair at times, but at the end of the day Hockey is simply a great teaching tool for your child to learn how to be successful at LIFE.

CHAPTER 20
THE PERFECT SEASON

One of the most gratifying seasons that I was ever involved in was coaching at the Pee Wee level. I found out early that this group of young players and parents were very special. During our training camp parent meeting I was surprised with the support that I was welcomed with. The parents and players of the camp were all there and excited to be a part of this team. I welcomed everyone to the camp and went right into my main topic for the meeting. I said these exact words. "I hate training camps or tryouts, because I always have to break some kid's heart and that is not why I chose to coach the game that has meant so much in my life.

I explained in detail how the evaluation process was going to work, and the evaluators that would be helping me make the team selections. I had 27 players trying out and because of numbers; we were only able to keep 13 skaters and 2 goalies. So I made it perfectly clear about everything that was going to happen. I had several parents thank me for the honest direct approach that I took during the meeting. We had exit meetings with every player to give them some real feedback. The players that I kept on the team got a very limited overview of their camp, just that they would be playing on our team this year. The unfortunate players that were sent to the house team were given some real feedback by me personally to give each player a good feeling about their tryout and some things that they could work on to better their game. I also let every player know that if there were parents that wanted to talk to me after the player meetings were complete I would make myself available. The Process went very smoothly and the parents I spoke to after were very understanding because of the difficult decisions we had to make.

After we selected the team, we immediately the following day had another team meeting with players and parents. We went over tournaments we wanted to go to, and the financial commitments and fundraising possibilities that were available to us. I am a big believer if you keep everyone involved as much as possible, they will have no time to bitch, complain or coach their kids from the sideline. As the Head coach of this team, with no kids of my own on the team, I at that time and only after the complete selection of the team, asked for some help from the parents as assistant coaches to help run the team. During the tryout process you cannot have any parents helping in any way to select the team; it just opens yourself up for criticism with regards to favoritism and pre selecting the players. This is not the perception you want to give to the group as a whole, and the player that you are hurting the most will be the player of the parent that is involved in any capacity. Ask your local organization for help if you don't have the contacts necessary to recruit your own impartial selection group. During our season, we focused on just getting better each week; the season was broken into 5 parts, and a 5th part being us playing our best hockey going into the playoffs. We finished the league in first place; we kept our thoughts only on the next game we had to play. Our team was constructed with quality goaltending, a solid blue line, and a very good forward core.

This group could play in both ends of the ice. Our Captain was a very small dedicated hard working center man, what he lacked in size he certainly made up with great heart and passion for the game. Before our playoffs, we decided as a team to dye all of our hair blonde, that is all except the coaches. The players hounded us to the point that we decide to join in, the deal was. "If we made it to provincials, the assistant coaches would also Dye their hair blonde, and if we won the Provincial championship, I then would Dye my hair blonde. This team building exercise became the focal point of our playoff run. The players were fortunate enough to have one of the moms that was a hairdresser and volunteered to dye all the boys' hair, the night before the playoffs.

What a ride, the players and the parents were all on board for a very long emotional ride to the Provincial championship game. This team was successful not because we were able to win some hockey games, but because we were a team, for the first time I was able to realize that this is what team means.

"Playing together for a common goal, with everyone pulling in the same direction"

Having the parents all supporting each other and the kids win or lose.
Doing activities away from the rink as a group and not having hockey as the main theme.

This group of special individuals I still keep in touch with today. A couple of players went on to play junior hockey, but most of them are now just finishing college or university and are all doing great in their chosen field. I somehow feel just maybe I had a small part in their success. That is why I continue to coach.

By the way, we lost the championship game in overtime and I would not trade in that experience for anything. As for dying my hair if we won the Provincials, I did it anyways as in my mind our team were Champion's, I didn't need a banner to prove it.